GAINing the Edge

AI Strategies for a Future-Ready Organization

Dr. Patrick Jones

OLYMPUS ACADEMY
PRESS

TABLE OF CONTENTS

INTRODUCTION

Welcome to a journey that will demystify artificial intelligence and show you how to harness its potential for your organization, your team, or even your own personal projects. Whether you're an executive curious about how AI can streamline operations or an individual intrigued by the possibilities of smart automation, this book aims to deliver practical, down-to-earth guidance you can start using right away. More importantly, it will do so without drowning you in convoluted jargon or overwhelming you with unrealistic promises. AI isn't a magic trick or a passing fad; it's a tool—one with remarkable capabilities that can fundamentally change how we work, innovate, and even think about problem-solving.

You might be wondering why there's another book on artificial intelligence. After all, plenty of resources already exist, many of which either veer into highly technical details or remain so conceptual that you're left wondering how they apply to real-world tasks. The inspiration for this book grew out of watching organizations struggle to strike that perfect balance between understanding AI's complexities and knowing how to make practical use of it. I've seen teams freeze up in the face of unfamiliar technology, terrified they'll adopt something they can't manage. I've also seen people leap in headfirst, only to be overwhelmed by data issues, privacy concerns, or unrealistic expectations. This book is an attempt to provide a roadmap that addresses both ends of the spectrum: the broader strategic questions and the day-to-day realities of turning AI ideas into practical solutions.

One of the key elements that makes this text different is the GAIN model, which stands for Ground Floor, Advance, Innovate, and New Horizons. It's a simple, yet powerful structure for thinking about AI adoption in stages. Ground Floor covers those first steps where organizations automate basic tasks—things that humans might have done manually for years. Advance is about ramping up efficiency and insight without completely overhauling core processes. Innovate takes AI further, transforming those processes in more fundamental ways. Then there's New Horizons, where AI actually enables entire new business models, products, or services that previously might have been unimaginable. This four-stage progression helps you see exactly where you are now and where you could be headed next, offering milestones and a sense of direction. You might find your team is still at Ground Floor with a single pilot project—or maybe you're already Innovating and looking to aim for a game-changing New Horizons initiative.

While this book outlines the GAIN model in detail, it doesn't treat AI adoption as a purely theoretical exercise. Much of what you'll read is designed to be as actionable as possible. From building a strategic roadmap to addressing security and privacy concerns, from building an AI-ready culture to measuring the return on your AI investments, each chapter aims to guide you through real steps you can take. To bring these principles to life, you'll also follow the story of Alex, a project manager at a company called 365 Strategies. Alex's experiences—both the wins and the stumbling blocks—will help illustrate how AI might be introduced in a typical organization, how team members react, and what happens when everyone leans in with curiosity and an open mind.

Alex starts off with only a faint idea of how AI might improve the way 365 Strategies operates. Initially, all they have is a hunch that tasks taking up too much time could be handled more efficiently. But like many of us, Alex isn't an engineer or a data scientist; the role is more about project oversight, communications, and ensuring that clients remain happy. This is precisely why Alex's journey is so valuable to follow. It shows that you don't need to be an expert in neural networks to spot opportunities for AI or to spearhead meaningful change. Over the course of the book, you'll watch as Alex gathers information, rallies different stakeholders, confronts skepticism, and learns—through trial and error—how to integrate AI successfully.

Right from the start, you'll see why the book is structured in five parts. The first part lays the groundwork, clarifying the essential building blocks of AI and shedding light on why it has captured so much global attention. Many people come to AI with preconceived notions formed by media buzz or sci-fi films, so getting the basics right is crucial. You'll learn not just the technical terms (presented in an approachable way) but also how AI actually works in everyday life. You might be surprised by the variety of applications already running quietly in the background— like fraud detection systems at your bank or predictive text suggestions on your phone. Knowing this sets the foundation for everything that follows.

After you're comfortable with the basics, Part II explores how to prepare for an AI project. In many organizations, this is where plans get derailed. People rush to experiment with AI-driven tools without clarifying why they need it, what data they have, or how they'll measure success. That's why the chapters on strategy, data management, and ethical considerations all appear before you dive into the GAIN model. By understanding how to build a roadmap and align AI efforts with your overall mission, you significantly raise your chances of success. You'll also see Alex wrestle with data quality and collaboration issues, highlighting that the real puzzle isn't just about training algorithms; it's about making sure the infrastructure and the organization itself are ready.

Part III, where the GAIN model is fully introduced, might be considered the heart of the book. You'll travel through the four stages—Ground Floor, Advance, Innovate, and New Horizons—seeing how each one builds on the last. At Ground Floor, AI automates simple, everyday tasks, helping teams feel more comfortable with something that can initially seem daunting. At Advance, AI steps up and starts offering deeper insights and process improvements. Once trust in these tools grows, Innovate becomes possible, as AI-powered solutions begin replacing old ways of working with more efficient, creative methods. Finally, New Horizons invites you to dream bigger about entirely new ventures or offerings. It's not just about optimization; it's about reimagining the scope of what you can do.

As the book continues, you'll move into Part IV, which tackles how to drive AI success at a larger scale. It's one thing to run a few pilots or introduce new technology into a single department. It's another to weave AI into the fabric of the entire organization, influencing everything from hiring decisions to long-term planning. This requires thoughtful project management, a culture that supports learning, and careful tracking of metrics. You'll see that the people side of AI can be just as challenging as the technical side, if not more. From overcoming resistance to forming cross-functional teams, these chapters offer a guide that goes beyond programming. They speak to the organizational changes required to sustain AI initiatives over time.

Finally, Part V sets its sights on the future, showing you how to maintain momentum and keep your eyes open for the next wave of AI innovations. Like any rapidly evolving technology, AI can seem intimidating. But the chapters here will frame that evolution as an opportunity rather than a threat. You'll see how an organization that regularly experiments with new tools, respects ethical boundaries, and invests in the growth of its people can carve out a meaningful, forward-looking role in the AI landscape. For many, this is a refreshing change from the doom-and-gloom headlines about robots taking all our jobs. A more measured view might see AI as neither a savior nor a destroyer, but a dynamic set of tools that can drive creativity, efficiency, and entirely new possibilities if harnessed responsibly.

Throughout the entire book, you'll keep returning to Alex at 365 Strategies. Alex's story underscores what this journey can look like for any of us who find ourselves tasked with championing a technology that few people fully understand at first. Maybe you'll identify with Alex's attempts to convince cautious colleagues, or maybe you'll relate to feeling intimidated by engineers who speak a language of equations and code. Whatever your background, the story makes the concepts tangible, illustrating how theory translates into real conversations, decisions, and breakthroughs.

By the end, the aim is for you to feel confident, not just in your understanding of AI, but in your capacity to lead or participate in AI initiatives at whatever scale is right for you. You'll have a roadmap for how to move forward—assessing your current state, determining the best stage of the GAIN model to target next, and charting the path to get there. You'll also have a sense of how to navigate everyday challenges, from privacy to skepticism to building a team that can handle the complexities AI often brings to the table.

It's important to note that this book doesn't pretend AI is easy. It doesn't claim to teach you how to write an algorithm that'll solve every business problem overnight. Instead, it focuses on providing enough context, strategy, and real-world insights that you can make informed decisions about when, where, and how to implement AI. That might mean starting small with a single pilot or forging a grand strategy for an entire enterprise. Either way, the guiding principle here is informed action—decisions that stem from an understanding of both the technical aspects and the human dimensions of change.

So, consider this introduction your invitation. If you've ever felt intrigued by AI but unsure where to begin, the pages that follow offer a clear, manageable path. If you're already in the thick of AI projects, you'll find practical tips and new angles on questions you may have been grappling with. And if you simply want to broaden your horizons and learn more about what AI can do, this book will give you that framework in a friendly, conversational style.

With that, you're ready to embark on a journey through the fundamentals of artificial intelligence, the nuances of implementation, and ultimately, the transformative potential that awaits you on the other side. Keep an open mind, stay curious, and don't worry if you're not a technical wizard. As you'll soon see, AI's true magic emerges when people with different skills and perspectives come together to approach problems in fresh, imaginative ways. And along the way, remember that the path to adopting AI isn't a sprint; it's a continuous evolution that rewards patience, creativity, and above all, a willingness to learn.

PART I
UNDERSTANDING AI AND ITS VALUE

WHAT IS AI AND WHY DOES IT MATTER?

A New Buzzword at 365 Strategies

Alex juggled a steaming cup of coffee in one hand and a half-eaten bagel in the other as they rushed to the morning meeting at 365 Strategies. Outside the conference room, a group of coworkers chatted about something that immediately caught Alex's attention: "AI might revolutionize how we write client proposals," one of them said, eyes lighting up with excitement. Another nodded and added, "We've been hearing all this buzz about machine learning and predictive analytics—it could be a game-changer."

Although Alex considered themselves reasonably tech-savvy, the term "AI" sounded a bit mysterious. Sure, they'd heard about chatbots, virtual assistants, and the occasional story about robots beating humans at board games, but how did any of that connect to day-to-day projects at 365 Strategies? And how could it possibly "revolutionize" the writing of client proposals?

Feeling both intrigued and a little out of the loop, Alex decided it was time to do some digging. Over the next couple of days, in between meetings and project deadlines, Alex pored over articles explaining artificial intelligence in plain language. They watched short videos about algorithms that learn from data, scrolled through social media where every startup seemed to brag about AI-driven solutions, and jotted down notes every time they stumbled on a new insight. The deeper Alex went, the more they realized that AI wasn't some distant, futuristic concept. It was already here, shaping everything from online shopping to healthcare diagnoses.

Yet a persistent question lingered in Alex's mind: What exactly is artificial intelligence, and why does everyone seem so convinced it's crucial for our future? Determined to find out, Alex set up a brief "AI

101" chat session with anyone at 365 Strategies who was interested. The turnout was surprisingly large. It seemed Alex wasn't the only one who wanted a clearer picture of what AI actually was, why it mattered, and how it could help the company. By the end of that week, Alex was ready to share some foundational insights—not only to satisfy their own curiosity but also to spark a conversation that would shape the firm's next steps.

What is AI and Why Does It Matter?

Artificial intelligence, often shortened to AI, is a field of computer science that focuses on creating machines or software that can mimic certain aspects of human intelligence. At its core, AI involves getting computers to learn from data, recognize patterns, make predictions, or even generate new ideas—all tasks we generally associate with thinking or problem-solving.

While AI used to be confined to research labs and sci-fi movies, it has quickly become part of everyday life. Have you ever used a smartphone app that guesses your next word in a text message? That's AI at work, using predictive algorithms to figure out what you might say next. Ever asked a voice assistant like Siri or Alexa for the weather report? That's another example. Even when you browse online shopping sites, AI systems are busy recommending products based on your past purchases or search history.

AI has gotten so much attention lately because it's no longer just theoretical. Thanks to advancements in computing power (our computers got faster and cheaper) and the rise of big data (we're generating more data than ever before), AI systems can now tackle tasks that once seemed impossible. They can diagnose diseases by scanning medical images, drive cars, or even help scientists discover new medicines. In business settings, AI can churn through massive datasets in seconds, spotting trends or anomalies a human might miss.

But beyond the flashy headlines, why does AI really matter to professionals like Alex, who are simply trying to do better work at 365 Strategies? The answer lies in two main benefits:

1. **Efficiency and Automation**: AI can handle repetitive, mundane tasks such as data entry or scheduling, freeing up time for people to focus on strategic or creative work.

2. **Deeper Insights**: AI can sift through huge amounts of information—like thousands of client proposals or hours of customer feedback—to find patterns and relationships that humans might overlook.

One way to think about AI is to imagine you're teaching a toddler how to recognize a cat. You show them many pictures of cats, saying "cat" each time. Over time, the toddler starts to form a mental model of what features make something look like a cat—maybe the pointy ears, whiskers, and tail. Eventually, they can spot a cat in a new photo they've never seen before. AI works similarly. Instead of a toddler, you have a computer program; instead of a few photos, you might have thousands. The more examples the system sees, the better it gets at recognizing patterns—whether those patterns are in images, text, or numbers.

This method—often called *machine learning*—is a major reason AI is so effective in real-world applications. Rather than relying on a predefined set of rules, AI algorithms learn from actual examples, allowing them to adapt to new information and improve over time.

When people hear the term "AI," they often picture futuristic robots that can talk and think exactly like humans. While movies have popularized that image, most real-world AI is far more specialized. A system designed to recommend songs based on your listening habits doesn't "understand" music the way a human does—it just recognizes patterns. Similarly, an AI that helps doctors spot tumors in X-ray scans doesn't fully grasp the concept of health or disease; it's just extremely good at detecting visual patterns that correlate with tumors.

In other words, the AI we use today is usually *narrow AI*, focused on a single task or problem. The idea of a general AI—one that can think and reason exactly like a human across various domains—remains in the realm of long-term research or science fiction.

For businesses, schools, or organizations, AI's power can translate into tangible benefits. Here are a few common examples:

- **Automation of Repetitive Tasks**: Companies can use AI to automate manual data entry, invoice processing, or basic customer support queries through chatbots.

- **Improved Decision-Making**: AI can analyze large datasets to predict market trends, identify potential risks, or recommend the best course of action.

- **Personalization**: Marketing teams can use AI to tailor content and recommendations to individual customers, improving engagement and satisfaction.

- **Predictive Analytics**: By learning from past data, AI can forecast sales, spot equipment failures before they happen, or help assign staff more effectively to different projects.

One of the main reasons AI is so sought after is its ability to handle tasks at a speed and scale that humans simply can't match. That's not to say it replaces human expertise. In fact, many experts believe the best results come from combining human intuition and creativity with AI's computational power.

Of course, AI also comes with its own set of challenges:

- **Data Requirements**: AI systems thrive on high-quality data. If your data is incomplete or riddled with errors, your AI outcomes will suffer.

- **Ethical Concerns**: Using AI responsibly involves questions about bias, privacy, and transparency. We'll explore this in later chapters.

- **Skill Gaps**: Organizations often need data-savvy people who understand both the business context and the technology enough to guide AI projects.

Still, these challenges haven't slowed AI's momentum. If anything, they highlight why understanding AI is crucial, so you can harness its potential responsibly and effectively.

Bringing AI Understanding Back to 365 Strategies

After a week of mini-research, chatting with coworkers, and even watching a few late-night videos explaining machine learning, Alex felt like a puzzle had finally started to come together. AI was no longer a distant concept found only in tech circles; it was a practical tool that could significantly improve day-to-day workflows. More importantly, Alex realized that 365 Strategies' discussion about using AI to "revolutionize client proposals" wasn't an exaggeration. AI could genuinely help the firm analyze past proposals, discover what worked best, and guide future writing in a more data-driven way.

Excited to share these insights, Alex organized a short "AI Basics" meetup with a few teammates who'd shown interest in the topic. Around a small conference table, Alex broke down the main points:

1. AI is about teaching computers to learn from examples.

2. It's not just about robots—it's about analyzing data to find patterns and make predictions.

3. Most importantly, it's practical and already being used in many parts of daily life.

As the team discussed potential uses at 365 Strategies, some fresh ideas surfaced. Maybe the firm could automate part of the research process for client proposals, feeding an AI system with historical data to pick out winning strategies. Or perhaps they could explore a chatbot to handle initial client questions. By the end of the meeting, everyone agreed on one thing: AI mattered because it had the potential to free them from tedious tasks and open the door to bigger, more impactful projects.

Stepping away from that discussion, Alex felt a newfound sense of confidence. The buzzword "AI" was no longer intimidating. Instead, it was an exciting frontier—one that 365 Strategies could approach with careful planning, open minds, and a willingness to experiment. Sure, there was still plenty to learn about ethical considerations, data requirements, and technical details, but Alex knew the journey had truly begun. And it all started with understanding what AI really is and why it's reshaping the world as we know it.

THE AI LANDSCAPE—WHERE WE ARE TODAY

Curiosity Meets Caution at 365 Strategies

With a fresh notebook in hand, Alex settled into a corner booth in the 365 Strategies break area. They were waiting for a quick chat with Jordan—their boss—about an exciting new proposal. After discovering what AI really was in the previous week, Alex had spent hours looking up real-world examples of artificial intelligence at work in various industries. Some of these examples were downright fascinating: hospitals using AI to catch diseases earlier, city planners using algorithms to ease traffic congestion, and even farmers monitoring crop health with camera-equipped drones.

But as Alex scribbled notes, Jordan arrived with a cautious smile. "So," Jordan began, "I hear you're putting together a briefing on AI. We're all for innovation, but I need to see how it ties back to real outcomes. How have other businesses used AI successfully?" Jordan tapped the table and leaned forward. "Numbers, case studies—things that show we're not just chasing a shiny new object."

That was the big question: Was AI truly transforming everyday work, or was it just overhyped tech speak? Alex suspected it was a bit of both. The articles Alex had read mentioned glowing success stories, but they also referenced many companies stalling after a pilot project. A balanced view seemed necessary, especially for Jordan, who wanted to try new ideas but also guard against wasted resources.

Determined to satisfy both curiosity and caution, Alex promised Jordan a short overview of AI's current landscape. Over the following days, Alex dived into examples from fields like healthcare, finance, retail, and even local government. In every corner of society, AI seemed to be taking root. The question now was: Which lessons could 365 Strategies learn from these diverse success stories—and which pitfalls should they avoid?

How AI Has Moved from Theory to Practice

Artificial intelligence is no longer reserved for Silicon Valley research labs or futuristic tech expos. It's everywhere—often working behind the scenes to power tools and services we use daily. Let's look at some broad ways AI has found its way into different industries:

Healthcare: Faster Diagnoses and Personalized Care

- **Medical Imaging**: Hospitals now use AI to scan X-rays, MRIs, or CT scans, flagging suspicious areas for further review by human doctors. Early results indicate that AI can spot tumors or fractures even earlier than some specialists, potentially leading to faster, more accurate diagnoses.

- **Virtual Health Assistants**: Some clinics use AI-powered chatbots to answer basic patient questions and schedule appointments. While not a replacement for doctors, these tools free up medical staff to focus on complex cases.

The lesson here? AI excels at analyzing large datasets (like thousands of patient records) to detect patterns or abnormalities. In a consulting environment like 365 Strategies, this same principle could help sift through large amounts of client data to find valuable insights, whether those insights concern budget overruns or untapped revenue opportunities.

Finance: Fraud Detection and Automated Advising

- **Fraud Monitoring**: Banks have long relied on rule-based systems to spot suspicious transactions. Now, AI-driven models can learn from each new case of fraud, adapting to changing criminal tactics more quickly than traditional methods ever could.

- **Robo-Advisors**: Services like Betterment or Wealthfront use algorithms to provide automated financial advice, adjusting investment portfolios to match a user's risk tolerance. While human advisors still play a crucial role, AI supports them by handling routine calculations.

For 365 Strategies, the takeaway is that AI doesn't replace human expertise in finance; it augments it. Consultants can similarly use AI-driven tools to detect anomalies in project spending or identify patterns in client investments that might benefit from reallocation.

Retail and Marketing: Personalization and Inventory Management

- **Product Recommendations**: If you've ever noticed an online store suggesting items "just for you," that's AI at work, learning from your browsing and purchase history.

- **Inventory Tracking**: In large warehouses, AI helps track stock levels, predict demand spikes, and reduce waste by keeping the right amount of product on hand at the right time.

365 Strategies could adapt similar logic to client engagement. By analyzing past proposals and project outcomes, an AI system might recommend new lines of service or marketing pitches specifically tailored to a client's history and industry sector.

Local Government: Smart Traffic and Resource Allocation

- **Traffic Control**: Several major cities have begun using real-time data from cameras and sensors to optimize traffic lights, reducing congestion during peak hours.

- **Resource Planning**: Local governments tap into AI to predict where services like waste collection or public safety patrols are most needed, making better use of limited budgets.

For a consulting firm, these examples demonstrate that AI can be a critical planning tool. Whether it's scheduling staff or allocating a marketing budget, predictive algorithms can help allocate resources more effectively.

Beyond large-scale deployments, AI is also part of everyday consumer tools. Voice assistants like Siri, Alexa, or Google Assistant use machine learning to recognize speech patterns, understand user intent, and improve responses over time. The next time you ask your device about the weather, you're tapping into some form of AI—one that's built on years of research, enormous datasets, and sophisticated neural networks.

It's easy to look at big-name companies and assume you need a massive budget to do anything meaningful with AI. That's not necessarily true. Cloud-based AI services now offer smaller organizations the ability to run advanced analytics without building huge data centers or hiring dozens of data scientists. Companies can pay for only the computing power they need, leveraging platforms like Amazon Web Services, Microsoft Azure, or Google Cloud.

Moreover, many AI tools come pre-built for specific tasks—like chatbots for customer service or fraud detection modules for e-commerce. This means you don't have to reinvent the wheel. Instead, you focus on customizing the tool for your organization's unique data and goals. Whether you're a three-person startup or a mid-sized consulting firm, AI can be molded to fit your operations as long as you choose projects that align with your needs and resources.

- **Pilot Projects**: Big ideas are great, but starting with a small pilot can help you see tangible benefits without sinking excessive time and money.

- **Clear Metrics**: AI projects should have a defined goal—like "reduce man-hours by 20% in invoice processing" or "increase lead conversion by 15%." Vague ambitions often lead to unclear outcomes.

- **Change Management**: AI might shift how people do their jobs, so organizations need training and open communication to address fear or confusion about new technologies.

This is exactly why leaders like Jordan, at 365 Strategies, remain both intrigued and cautious. The success stories are real, but they hinge on careful planning, realistic goals, and a willingness to adapt to change.

New Ideas for 365 Strategies

A few days later, Alex presented a concise report to Jordan, highlighting key case studies where AI made a real difference. Alex showed how medical systems had improved patient care, how banks caught fraud more effectively, and how local governments streamlined operations. Then, they connected the dots: "We're not building a self-driving car here," Alex said with a grin, "but these examples show that AI can solve our day-to-day challenges in a similarly targeted, practical way."

Jordan nodded, flipping through the summaries. "Okay, so it's more than hype," Jordan admitted. "But what's our entry point? How does a consulting firm like ours jump in without overcommitting?"

Smiling, Alex explained a few short-term possibilities:

- **Automating Routine Tasks**: For instance, data entry or basic analysis of large sets of project documents.

- **Predictive Insights**: Using AI to identify trends in client needs or market changes before they become big issues.

- **Client Engagement**: Creating a simple chatbot or automated support tool to handle common queries or gather initial information before a human consultant steps in.

As the meeting concluded, Jordan looked genuinely impressed. "Let's start small," Jordan proposed. "Show me a pilot project where we can measure the impact clearly. If it works, we'll scale up."

Leaving the room, Alex felt a surge of confidence. It was clear that AI's impact was already massive in many industries—and 365 Strategies didn't have to be a tech giant to benefit. All it took was careful planning, a clear understanding of the firm's objectives, and the ability to learn from the successes (and pitfalls) others had experienced. Alex couldn't wait to see how these insights would shape the company's roadmap in the coming weeks.

THE BUSINESS CASE FOR AI

Justifying the Investment at 365 Strategies

Alex sifted through a stack of papers, half of them old project reports and the other half articles about AI breakthroughs. The goal was straightforward yet challenging: to convince the leadership team at 365 Strategies that investing in an AI-driven analytics tool could pay off. Sure, the team had already seen examples of AI at work in other companies, but how would it make a tangible difference here? And more importantly, how would Alex translate that potential into a persuasive financial case?

One morning, Alex received an email from Jordan, the boss, that read: "Can you put together a brief proposal? Show me the ROI—numbers if possible—and also any intangible benefits we might gain from being seen as a more innovative firm." Feeling a mix of excitement and pressure, Alex spent the next few days collecting data on how much time was currently spent on repetitive tasks, how many errors were creeping into certain manual processes, and how clients perceived 365 Strategies' tech-savviness. As Alex wove these details into a draft proposal, it became clear that while some benefits could be easily measured—like the time saved in data entry—others, such as "brand perception," didn't fit neatly into a spreadsheet.

Still, Alex knew that leaders at 365 Strategies liked seeing hard facts. If the proposal lacked concrete numbers, it would be tough to justify the costs. On the other hand, ignoring those more abstract "image-boosting" perks would skip a key part of AI's value. Striking the right balance was going to be tricky.

Making the Business Case for AI

Building a compelling business case for AI involves more than quoting flashy statistics or jumping on the latest tech trend. It requires a clear explanation of how AI supports the organization's strategic goals and a realistic appraisal of both the tangible and intangible benefits. Below are some straightforward steps to follow when you need to convince stakeholders to invest in AI:

1. Start with Tangible, Measurable Returns

- **Cost Savings and Efficiency**: One of the easiest ways to gain buy-in is to show how AI can reduce operational expenses. For example, if employees spend 10 hours a week on manual data entry, and a new AI tool can cut that time in half, you can translate those saved hours into direct cost savings.

- **Fewer Errors**: Mistakes in data entry or repetitive tasks can be expensive and time-consuming to fix. An AI system that catches errors early or automates those tasks altogether can lead to measurable savings in rework and client dissatisfaction.

- **Faster Turnaround Times**: If your team can produce reports or analyses more quickly, that might translate to happier clients or shorter project timelines. You can estimate how many days a project might be shortened, then tie that to potential revenue boosts or cost reductions.

Presenting such numbers helps stakeholders see that AI isn't just a futuristic gamble—it can have a real, positive effect on the bottom line.

2. Highlight Strategic and Competitive Advantages

- **Innovation and Market Position**: Using AI can elevate a company's reputation, marking it as forward-thinking or cutting edge. While "brand perception" can be tough to quantify, it can attract bigger clients, better talent, and more media attention.

- **Staying Ahead of Competitors**: If your competitors are already leveraging AI for predictive insights or advanced customer interactions, you risk falling behind. Sometimes, the business case for AI is about not losing ground in a quickly evolving market.

When making this argument, it helps to present industry examples or case studies, showing how similar companies used AI to achieve a competitive edge.

3. Consider Intangible Benefits

While the numbers may get all the attention, intangible benefits can be just as important:

- **Employee Satisfaction**: By automating mundane tasks, you free people to focus on more creative or strategic work, which can boost morale and reduce turnover.

- **Collaboration**: AI often requires bringing teams together—IT, operations, marketing—fostering a culture of collaboration that can improve the entire organization's performance.

- **Client Trust and Loyalty**: If clients see you embracing advanced tools, they may trust your capacity for innovation, leading to stronger partnerships.

Acknowledge these benefits in your proposal, even if you can't put them all in a neat spreadsheet. They can shape the company's long-term growth in ways that strictly financial metrics might overlook.

4. Address Costs and Risks Honestly

No one wants to be blindsided by hidden expenses. Outline the potential costs:

- **Licensing or Subscription Fees**: AI platforms can charge based on the number of users or the amount of data processed.

- **Implementation and Integration**: You may need outside consultants or in-house staff to set up and customize AI tools.

- **Ongoing Training and Maintenance**: AI models aren't static; they require updates, and staff need training to interpret results correctly.

Also, be upfront about risks, such as data quality issues or over-reliance on AI insights without human judgment. By addressing these concerns proactively, you build credibility and show stakeholders you've done your homework.

5. Show Clear Metrics for Success

Finally, define how you'll measure whether the AI investment is successful. This might include:

- **Time Saved**: Fewer hours spent on manual tasks each week.
- **Error Rate Reduction**: A measurable drop in mistakes or rework.
- **Customer Satisfaction Scores**: An increase in how clients rate your services or products.
- **Project Throughput**: The ability to handle more projects without adding extra staff.

These metrics give everyone a way to evaluate the AI project's performance, making further investment decisions smoother down the line.

A Proposal to Win Hearts and Minds

After days of number crunching and deliberating over intangible benefits, Alex pulled together a short proposal for the leadership team at 365 Strategies. The document led with some eye-catching figures—calculations showing that an AI-driven analytics tool could reduce certain repetitive tasks by 30%, resulting in several thousands of dollars saved annually. Next, Alex highlighted the potential for the firm to market itself as more cutting-edge. "We often pitch ourselves as innovators,"

Alex wrote. "Here's a chance to walk the talk—showing clients that we use the same advanced methods we recommend to them."

When it came to brand perception, Alex admitted it was tricky to put a dollar figure on something like "innovative reputation." Instead, the proposal included anecdotal evidence from past client surveys and a few projections of how being known for AI adoption could lead to higher-value contracts. It wasn't a perfect science, but Alex hoped it would at least open the team's eyes to the broader possibilities.

Finally, Alex ended the document by listing potential costs—everything from the software subscription to the time needed for staff training. In doing so, Alex made it clear that while AI had significant potential, it wasn't a magic wand. It required resources and commitment to succeed. Upon reviewing the proposal, Jordan nodded thoughtfully. "This looks promising. You've given us concrete numbers to chew on, plus some interesting long-term benefits. Let's schedule a broader discussion with finance and operations to see how this might fit our strategic roadmap."

Walking out of Jordan's office, proposal in hand, Alex felt a sense of relief and accomplishment. Putting together a business case for AI wasn't about making inflated promises; it was about showing how real improvements—both financial and intangible—could come from integrating AI into 365 Strategies' operations. And if everything went well, the firm wouldn't just save money; it would also cement its place as an organization that embraced the future without losing sight of the practical bottom line.

AI BASICS FOR EVERYONE— DEMYSTIFYING TECH JARGON

Lunchtime Crash Course

Alex couldn't help but smile at the crowd gathering around the conference table during lunch hour. The previous week, Alex had casually mentioned hosting an "AI Basics" session—just a friendly get-together to help demystify the buzzwords flying around 365 Strategies. To Alex's surprise, the event drew a mix of people: from seasoned consultants to administrative staff, all curious about what terms like "machine learning" and "neural networks" actually meant. Some even admitted they hadn't touched math since high school and felt slightly intimidated by technical talk.

While arranging bagels and fresh coffee, Alex sensed the group's nervous excitement. Everyone was intrigued by AI, but no one wanted to appear lost or behind the times. In many ways, Alex felt the same. Despite immersing themselves in AI projects, they still found certain jargon puzzling. "If we're going to embrace this technology," Alex thought, "we need to speak a common language that makes sense to everyone—from top executives to new interns."

With that in mind, Alex kicked off the lunch-and-learn by acknowledging a shared anxiety: "Let's be honest—AI jargon can sound scary. But I promise it's not rocket science. We'll break it down so that by the end of this session, terms like 'machine learning' and 'neural networks' will feel a lot more comfortable."

Breaking Down Common AI Terms

Artificial intelligence is a field filled with fancy-sounding words that can deter even the most curious learners. But most of these terms describe straightforward concepts when explained with everyday analogies. Below are some key terms, each introduced in plain, friendly language.

Machine Learning: Learning by Example

What it is:
Machine learning is the process by which a computer program learns from data rather than following fixed, unchanging rules. Think of it like teaching a child to recognize a dog: you show them lots of pictures of dogs, and over time they pick up the features that define "dog." The child isn't memorizing each picture; they're learning the general characteristics of dog-ness—four legs, fur, a certain snout shape. Then, when they see a new picture of a dog, they can identify it correctly.

Why it matters:
In the business world, machine learning helps with tasks like predicting sales trends, flagging fraud, or recommending new products to customers. It's basically a pattern-recognition engine. Once you feed it the right examples, it can make surprisingly accurate guesses about new, unseen data.

Neural Networks: Layers of "Virtual Neurons"

What it is:
Neural networks are a specific type of machine learning model inspired by the human brain. They're made up of layers of "nodes" or "neurons," each layer passing information to the next. Picture a big, layered sandwich: each layer adds its own flavor before handing it off to the next layer.

In a neural network, the first layer might pick out simple features—like edges or shapes if you're analyzing images—while deeper layers look for more complex patterns. That's why the term "deep learning" often comes up: the more layers you add, the deeper your network, and the more complex patterns it can learn.

Why it matters:
Neural networks power many of the most impressive AI feats: from image recognition to language translation. If you've ever used a voice assistant like Siri or asked Google to translate a phrase, you've benefited from neural network magic behind the scenes.

Natural Language Processing (NLP): Helping Computers Understand Text

What it is:
NLP is the area of AI focused on how computers interpret human language in text or speech. It's the reason your phone can suggest words as you type, or why a chatbot can (sometimes) hold a decent conversation.

Why it matters:
NLP could mean scanning large batches of client documents or past proposals to find relevant information. It might also power a question-and-answer system for employees looking up company policies. Essentially, NLP is about teaching AI to read, write, and speak like a human—though it's still far from perfect.

Supervised vs. Unsupervised Learning

Supervised Learning:
In supervised learning, you feed the AI labeled examples—like bank transactions tagged as "fraudulent" or "legitimate"—so it can learn to classify new, unlabeled examples. It's akin to showing a toddler flashcards with the word "cat" on them each time a cat appears. Over time, the system forms an understanding that "features x, y, and z" point to one label or another.

Unsupervised Learning:
Here, no labels exist. You just give the AI a bunch of data, and it tries to find hidden patterns or clusters. Think of it like handing a kid a big pile

of toys without telling them which is which. They might group them by color, size, or shape, noticing patterns that weren't obvious before.

Why it matters:
Supervised learning might help classify successful project proposals vs. unsuccessful ones. Unsupervised learning could help uncover new client segments or unexpected commonalities in data, opening the door to fresh business strategies.

Overfitting: Teaching a Parrot

One more concept is overfitting, or when a model learns the training data too well—almost like it's memorizing every detail rather than learning general patterns. This is like teaching a parrot to repeat a phrase without understanding it. The parrot sounds smart, but it can't actually apply that phrase in a new context. Overfitting in AI means the model might perform brilliantly on the data it's already seen, but flounder when faced with new information.

Simplifying the Tech Talk: Useful Analogies

To make these concepts stick, use simple analogies:

- **Machine Learning**: Like a child learning to recognize animals by seeing lots of pictures.

- **Neural Networks**: Layers of insight—think of it as a layered sandwich.

- **NLP**: Teaching a computer to read, write, and talk, somewhat like an artificial pen pal.

- **Supervised vs. Unsupervised**: Think flashcards with answers vs. a game of sorting toys by color or size.

These visuals made it easier—regardless of their technical background—to "see" what AI was doing.

From Buzzwords to Real Understanding

By the end of the lunch-and-learn, the once-quiet room was abuzz with conversation. Tony from Operations asked if a supervised model could help predict staffing needs for large projects. Rachel from Marketing wondered how NLP could sift through client feedback to pinpoint key trends. Even folks from finance saw an opportunity to use machine learning for forecasting budgets.

Alex looked around, pleased with how enthusiastic everyone seemed. Gone was the initial hesitation around jargon. In its place was a sense of shared excitement and a willingness to explore practical applications. The session had shown that you don't need a computer science degree to grasp the basics of AI; you just need the right analogies and an open mind.

Over the next few days, Alex noticed more people casually dropping AI terms around the office. Rachel joked that she'd "trained a supervised model" on her kids by showing them what not to do. Tony compared overfitting to memorizing test answers without truly learning the subject. Even Jordan, who had been cautious about AI projects, asked Alex if a neural network might one day analyze 365 Strategies' proposals in real time.

This renewed energy around AI set the stage for deeper conversations about how to actually implement these technologies—discussions about data, ethics, security, and scaling solutions to meet different departments' needs. Alex realized the importance of that afternoon session: by replacing confusing buzzwords with real-world examples, the team had transformed AI from a distant concept into a tool they felt empowered to experiment with.

As Alex packed up the leftover bagels, they couldn't help but feel optimistic. Sure, there was still a lot to learn, but at least the basics were now out in the open, no longer hidden behind acronyms or technical jargon. And that was the whole point—if AI was going to reshape the way 365 Strategies worked, everyone needed to understand the foundation first. Now, they had the common language and excitement to begin building on that foundation together.

PART II: PREPARING FOR AI IMPLEMENTATION

BUILDING THE AI STRATEGY ROADMAP

Juggling Department Demands

Alex stood at the whiteboard in a small meeting room at 365 Strategies, wrestling with an ever-expanding list of AI project ideas. Finance wanted to automate invoices for cost savings. Marketing dreamed of a chatbot to wow clients. Operations suggested a predictive model to streamline project schedules. HR proposed an AI-based recruitment tool to sift through thousands of resumes efficiently.

On paper, each idea sounded wonderful. But as Alex scribbled them all down, the reality sank in: there weren't enough resources—time, budget, or personnel—to tackle everything at once. Worse, if these projects weren't aligned with 365 Strategies' broader goals, they might end up as disjointed experiments rather than a cohesive strategy.

Recognizing this challenge, Alex called a quick "vision meeting" with representatives from each department. "We all want AI to make our lives easier and our company more competitive," Alex began, "but how do we decide which initiatives come first? And how do we ensure they don't conflict or duplicate effort?"

Jordan, the boss, raised an eyebrow. "That's the question," he said. "We need an actual roadmap—one that ties each project to our bigger picture. Otherwise, it's just random tech for tech's sake."

Over the next few days, Alex dived into reading about strategic planning for AI, hoping to find a framework that could help 365 Strategies prioritize, allocate resources, and set realistic timelines. It wasn't about saying "no" to good ideas, but rather about mapping them onto a logical sequence that aligned with the company's vision.

Crafting an Effective AI Roadmap

When organizations first get excited about AI, it's tempting to jump in with both feet—picking projects left and right. But successful AI adoption demands more than wish lists. It needs a roadmap that integrates goals, resources, timelines, and measurable outcomes. Below are steps to build such a roadmap, ensuring AI projects advance an organization's overarching vision rather than scattering efforts.

1. Align AI with Organizational Goals

Start by looking at the big picture: what are the company's strategic priorities? Are you aiming to:

- **Improve Customer Satisfaction** (e.g., faster support, personalized services)

- **Enhance Operational Efficiency** (e.g., cutting repetitive tasks, reducing costs)

- **Discover New Revenue Streams** (e.g., launching data-driven products)

- **Strengthen Brand Image** (e.g., positioning your firm as an industry innovator)

List these goals explicitly, then tie each AI idea back to at least one. This alignment avoids the trap of implementing AI just because it's trendy. Instead, every initiative serves a larger mission—creating a clear reason for stakeholders to support it.

2. Assess Readiness and Resources

Not every organization is ready to adopt advanced AI solutions from day one. Consider your current infrastructure, data quality, and internal skill sets.

- **Data Quality**: If your data is scattered or outdated, you may need a data-cleaning initiative before you can effectively deploy AI.

- **Infrastructure**: Do you have the necessary software and hardware to support AI tools? This might mean cloud services or on-premises systems robust enough for machine learning workloads.

- **Skill Gaps**: AI projects often require data scientists, machine learning engineers, or other specialized roles. If you don't have them, will you train existing staff or hire new talent?

By understanding these constraints, you avoid launching ambitious projects only to realize mid-way that you lack the tools or expertise.

3. Prioritize Based on Value and Feasibility

Once you align projects with goals and assess internal readiness, it's time to weigh them in terms of potential impact versus complexity:

- **High-Value, Low-Complexity**: These are quick wins. For instance, using an off-the-shelf tool to automate invoice processing might yield immediate cost savings without a massive technical lift.

- **High-Value, High-Complexity**: Some initiatives could transform the company—like a predictive analytics engine to forecast client demand. However, these may require significant investment in data management and specialized talent.

- **Low-Value, Low-Complexity**: Consider whether small gains justify the effort. Such projects can be postponed if resources are tight.

- **Low-Value, High-Complexity**: Likely not worth doing unless they support a critical aspect of your mission.

This matrix (Value vs. Feasibility) helps you rank projects logically, preventing energy from being drained by low-impact ideas or paralyzing complexity.

4. Map Out Timelines and Dependencies

Every project depends on something—be it clean data, a certain budget, or coordination between departments. A good AI roadmap spells out these dependencies. For example, you might start with simpler, data-cleaning tasks (Phase 1), then move to an AI-powered chatbot once the customer data is organized (Phase 2), and only then tackle advanced analytics for predictive scheduling (Phase 3).

Set realistic milestones and key performance indicators (KPIs) for each phase. For instance:

- **Phase 1**: Implement invoice automation. KPI: Reduce manual invoicing time by 50% within six months.

- **Phase 2**: Deploy chatbot for customer queries. KPI: Increase first-response rate by 80% by the end of the year.

- **Phase 3**: Launch predictive scheduling model. KPI: Decrease project overruns by 30% in the following year.

Clear timelines and goals give everyone a shared understanding of what success looks like and when they can expect tangible results.

5. Foster Collaboration and Communication

An AI roadmap isn't just a document; it's a living plan that requires continuous input from multiple teams. Finance might care about ROI, Marketing might need a slick user interface, and Operations might want the project workflow to remain efficient. Establish a cross-functional committee or steering group that meets regularly to review progress, surface issues, and adjust timelines as needed.

Also, keep an open channel of communication with all stakeholders, from top leadership to end-users. Regular updates, simple dashboards showing progress, and an open forum for questions can maintain enthusiasm and transparency.

6. Review, Learn, and Iterate

No roadmap is set in stone. As you complete AI projects, you'll learn what works (and what doesn't). Use these insights to refine future initiatives. Did the invoice automation bring fewer benefits than anticipated? Maybe you need to tweak the approach or shift resources to higher-impact areas. Agile organizations treat the roadmap as a cycle of continuous improvement rather than a one-and-done plan.

Uniting 365 Strategies

After immersing in strategy articles and talking to various department heads, Alex finally convened a workshop where each team could pitch their AI priorities. Some wanted quick wins, like automating routine tasks. Others had grand visions that would likely require a year of data cleanup and new hires.

Using the value-versus-feasibility approach, Alex helped them rank these ideas. Finance's invoice automation emerged as a strong contender for Phase 1: high payoff, relatively straightforward tech. Marketing's chatbot ambitions came in a bit later—still a valuable project, but it required a cleaner database of client interactions. The predictive scheduling model for Operations took shape as a longer-term initiative, given the need for more sophisticated analytics and training staff to trust an AI's scheduling suggestions.

During the workshop, tension arose when each department championed its own project as "the most urgent." Yet, with the roadmap in hand, Alex guided them to see how staggering these efforts made sense. "If we try everything at once," Alex pointed out, "we risk burning out our resources and ending up with half-baked implementations."

Jordan nodded in agreement, adding, "We're not saying 'no' to any idea. We're saying 'in time, with the right prep.'" This perspective helped calm the room. By the end of the session, the group had sketched out a six-month, one-year, and two-year AI timeline, linking each project to a broader organizational goal—cost savings, client satisfaction, or brand innovation.

Leaving the meeting, Alex felt a sense of relief and accomplishment. Crafting the roadmap wasn't just about choosing technologies; it was about balancing needs, managing expectations, and forging a united path forward. While there was still plenty of work ahead—budgets to secure, staff to train, data to prep—the team now had a clear direction. For the first time, the excitement about AI felt purposeful rather than scattered. And that, Alex realized, was the real power of a well-planned strategy: it harnessed everyone's enthusiasm and channeled it toward meaningful, coordinated progress.

MANAGING DATA AND INFRASTRUCTURE

A Tangled Web of Spreadsheets

Alex leaned back in their desk chair, staring at a screen filled with half-finished spreadsheets. Each document came from a different department at 365 Strategies—Marketing data in one corner, Operations logs in another, scattered finance records somewhere in the mix. Ideally, all this information could feed into an AI system that would spot trends and deliver real-time insights. But in practice, the data was inconsistent, incomplete, and sometimes just plain messy.

One morning, Alex attempted to merge some of these spreadsheets, hoping to get a baseline view of project budgets across departments. Within minutes, error messages popped up. Columns with mismatched names, date formats that varied wildly, and a tangle of missing fields rendered the process borderline impossible. Even worse, sensitive client information was mixed in, raising alarms about privacy and compliance.

Slightly frustrated but determined, Alex scheduled a meeting with two key allies: Priya from IT and Chantal from the legal team. Priya was the infrastructure expert, well-versed in data storage solutions and pipelines. Chantal understood the ins and outs of privacy regulations like GDPR, ensuring no lines were crossed when handling personal data. Alex's goal? To get everyone on the same page about data management and to figure out how to build a solid foundation for the company's budding AI projects.

Building a Solid Data Foundation

No matter how powerful an AI algorithm is, it can only be as good as the data it learns from. Messy, incomplete, or poorly secured data can derail even the most promising AI project. Below are the essential considerations for managing data and infrastructure in a way that sets AI initiatives up for success.

1. Data Collection and Centralization

- **Identify Data Sources**: The first step is to list out all the places where data lives: spreadsheets, CRM systems, cloud storage, or even paper documents.

- **Consolidate into a Single Repository**: A data warehouse or a data lake can serve as a centralized hub, ensuring everyone pulls information from the same source. This might mean migrating files to a cloud platform or setting up a dedicated server on-premises.

- **Consistency and Naming Conventions**: Decide on uniform naming conventions for files, folders, and database fields. Even simple rules, like using the same date format or labeling client records consistently, can save headaches later on.

Data silos—where each department hoards its own separate data— prevent a holistic view of the business. By consolidating everything into a well-organized repository, you pave the way for AI systems to analyze data comprehensively.

2. Data Cleaning and Quality Control

Once data is collected in one place, the next challenge is quality:

- **Remove Duplicates and Fill Missing Fields**: Systems like ETL (Extract, Transform, Load) can automate part of this, but human oversight is often needed to interpret ambiguous entries or reconcile conflicting records.

- **Standardize Formats**: Align date formats, measurement units, and naming conventions across different datasets. This uniformity prevents errors when the AI model attempts to combine fields.

- **Validation Rules**: Set up rules or scripts that flag suspicious entries—like a negative quantity for inventory or an implausible date of birth.

Quality data isn't just about making the AI's job easier; it's also about ensuring trustworthy results. If your training data is riddled with inaccuracies, the AI model's predictions or recommendations will be, too.

3. Privacy and Compliance

With regulations like GDPR and various local data protection laws, handling personal or sensitive information comes with responsibilities:

- **Lawful Basis for Data Use**: Ensure you have a valid reason for collecting and processing personal data. If you rely on user consent, be prepared to remove their data if they opt out.

- **Anonymization and Pseudonymization**: Techniques like anonymizing data (removing direct identifiers) or using pseudonyms instead of real names can limit privacy risks while still letting AI glean insights.

- **Access Controls**: Not everyone needs access to raw data. Some employees only need aggregated reports. Minimizing the number of people with full access lowers the risk of breaches.

Prioritizing privacy early not only keeps you compliant but also builds trust among clients and staff who might be wary of extensive data collection.

4. Infrastructure Considerations

Deciding how and where to store and process data is crucial:

- **On-Premises vs. Cloud**: On-premises solutions can offer full control but require more upfront costs and maintenance. Cloud solutions provide flexibility and often come with built-in AI services, but you rely on an external provider.

- **Scalability**: As your data grows, your infrastructure should scale without leading to downtime or excessive costs. Hybrid approaches—storing sensitive data on-premises while using the cloud for less sensitive analytics—can offer a balance of control and elasticity.

- **Security Measures**: Encryption at rest and in transit, regular backups, and network monitoring are baseline requirements. With AI models, also consider security around the model itself (like adversarial attacks that feed malicious data to skew results).

5. Building a Data Pipeline

Think of a data pipeline as the path data takes from raw collection to final insights:

1. **Ingestion**: Bringing data in from multiple sources (spreadsheets, databases, APIs).

2. **Processing/Transformation**: Cleaning and structuring the data—this might involve scripts or automated tools.

3. **Storage**: Placing the refined data into a warehouse or lake.

4. **Analysis and Modeling**: Feeding the stored data into AI or analytics tools.

5. **Feedback Loop**: Monitoring results, spotting errors, and refining the pipeline so that data remains accurate and up to date.

A well-designed pipeline ensures that as new data arrives, it's automatically validated and integrated, keeping the AI system's insights fresh and reliable.

6. Organizational Readiness and Culture

Finally, data management isn't purely technical. Successful AI adoption requires a culture that respects and understands data. This might include:

- **Training**: Teaching staff the basics of data handling and the importance of consistent record-keeping.

- **Ownership**: Assigning clear responsibility for data quality within each department.

- **Policies and Governance**: Establishing rules about what data is collected, how long it's kept, and who can access it.

By making data stewardship a shared value, you reduce the risk of "garbage in, garbage out" and strengthen the foundation upon which AI can flourish.

Bridging IT and Legal Realities

After their meeting with Priya (IT) and Chantal (Legal), Alex realized just how intertwined technical and legal concerns were. Priya explained the architectural options: a cloud-based solution that would provide agility but raise questions about third-party data storage, or an on-premises approach that demanded significant upfront investment in servers and maintenance. Chantal reminded them that any system chosen must handle customer data with care—especially EU-based clients subject to GDPR rules.

Armed with these insights, Alex began mapping out a data strategy for 365 Strategies. Step one was gathering department leads to figure out where data already existed and what shape it was in. It wasn't a glamorous process—scrolling through old folders, renaming files for consistency, and trimming obvious duplicates—but it laid the groundwork for the next phase of the AI roadmap. "We can't deploy fancy algorithms on a shaky foundation," Alex told the team. "Let's fix the house before inviting all these new AI projects in."

Along the way, Alex hit some stumbling blocks. A chunk of client records had come from a legacy system with no consistent format.

Operations data was sometimes stored locally on personal laptops. And a few employees balked at the new guidelines, complaining they didn't have time to rename files or fill in missing data. Patiently, Alex explained how these short-term efforts would save countless hours in the long run and strengthen security. Gradually, people came around, especially after seeing how even basic data cleansing improved reporting accuracy.

At the next leadership check-in, Jordan asked, "Are we any closer to rolling out that predictive analytics tool for scheduling?" Alex responded candidly: "We're getting there. Right now, we're building the foundation—making sure our data is usable and compliant. Once that's in place, the AI system will have reliable info to learn from, and we won't be dealing with nasty surprises later." Jordan nodded, satisfied with the logic. The team was finally seeing that managing data and infrastructure wasn't a bottleneck; it was an enabler.

Heading back to their desk, Alex felt a renewed sense of purpose. While data management could be tedious, each cleanup step and privacy safeguard brought 365 Strategies closer to the day when AI would seamlessly analyze data and guide smart decisions. It was a reminder that real progress in AI often starts with the unglamorous work of organizing information and respecting privacy—because only then can an organization harness AI's insights with clarity, confidence, and integrity.

SECURITY, PRIVACY, AND ETHICAL CONSIDERATIONS

A Sensitive Data Dilemma

Alex drummed their fingers on the conference room table, staring at a freshly printed proposal for a new AI pilot. The idea sounded promising: a tool that could analyze customer engagement data and help 365 Strategies offer personalized services. However, one big issue stuck out: the proposal called for access to a trove of sensitive client information, including some personal details that raised immediate red flags about privacy.

Before scheduling a meeting with the IT and legal teams, Alex did a quick mental checklist. Could we anonymize the data? Possibly, but would that limit the AI's usefulness? Did we have client consent? Unclear—some of the data had come from older contracts where privacy clauses weren't crystal clear. What if the tool got breached? That could erode the trust clients placed in 365 Strategies and spark legal troubles.

As Alex gathered notes, the door swung open. Jordan, the boss, walked in. "I hear we've got a potentially game-changing AI project here," Jordan said, scanning the proposal. "But you look worried."

Alex sighed. "It's exciting on paper, but we're dealing with personal data. If we're not careful, we could cross ethical lines or even break privacy laws."

Jordan nodded, sliding the proposal back across the table. "Let's figure out how to do it right. I need your input on the risks, the ethical angle, and the security measures. We want innovation, but not at the cost of trust."

Thus began Alex's deep dive into the interconnected world of security, privacy, and ethics—an aspect of AI that demanded more than just technical know-how. It required a moral and legal compass as well.

Balancing Ethics, Security, and Privacy in AI

Artificial intelligence brings enormous potential, but it also poses new kinds of risks. If a model trains on biased data, it can unintentionally discriminate. If data isn't secured, a breach can compromise sensitive information. If we don't handle personal details responsibly, we violate privacy laws and lose the public's trust. Below are the key areas any organization must address when handling AI projects.

1. Fairness and Bias

- **Why It Matters**: AI systems learn from historical data, which can contain hidden biases. If past hiring data favored certain demographic groups, an AI-driven recruitment tool might replicate or worsen that bias.

- **What to Do**:

    o **Diverse Training Data**: Strive for datasets that reflect a wide range of demographics, reducing the risk of skewed outcomes.

    o **Regular Audits**: Test your models for bias by checking whether they produce unequal results for different groups.

    o **Transparency and Oversight**: Involve stakeholders from various backgrounds to review AI projects, ensuring multiple perspectives catch potential biases early.

2. Data Privacy and Compliance

- **Why It Matters**: Laws like GDPR and other data protection regulations impose strict rules on collecting, storing, and processing personal information. Failure to comply can lead to hefty fines and damaged reputations.

- **What to Do**:

  - **Obtain Consent**: For personal data, ensure users have opted in and can opt out.

  - **Minimize Data Collection**: Don't gather more info than you need. If possible, anonymize data.

  - **Robust Access Controls**: Limit who can see raw data. The fewer eyes on sensitive information, the better.

3. Security Against Cyber Threats

- **Why It Matters**: AI tools often require large amounts of data, making them attractive targets for hackers. A breach can expose personal info, trade secrets, or entire databases.

- **What to Do**:

  - **Encrypt Data at Rest and in Transit**: Ensure that data is scrambled whether it's stored or traveling across a network.

  - **Implement Strong Authentication**: Multi-factor authentication for accounts that access AI systems or data.

  - **Monitor for Suspicious Activity**: Use intrusion detection systems, penetration tests, and logs that flag unusual data access.

4. Ethical Frameworks and Accountability

- **Why It Matters**: AI isn't purely technical; it influences human lives and decisions. Organizations that adopt AI must ask not just "Can we do this?" but "Should we?"

- **What to Do**:

  - **Create an Ethics Committee**: This group can review AI proposals, examining them for ethical pitfalls such as discrimination or potential harm to vulnerable communities.

  - **Develop Clear Guidelines**: Document how data should be used, what types of models are acceptable, and what oversight measures are in place.

  - **Lead with Transparency**: Communicate openly with clients and users about how and why you're using AI. Explain the benefits—and the safeguards.

5. Building User Trust

- **Why It Matters**: AI's success hinges on trust. Employees need to trust AI insights, and customers must trust the organization to handle their data responsibly.

- **What to Do**:

  - **Human-in-the-Loop Systems**: Let humans oversee critical decisions, such as final approvals or edge cases.

  - **Explainable AI**: Whenever possible, choose algorithms that can provide reasons for their outputs, making them less of a "black box."

  - **Training and Education**: Host internal sessions (similar to Alex's lunch-and-learns) to raise awareness. Educated teams are less likely to mishandle data or misuse AI.

6. Handling Breaches and Incidents

Even with precautions, breaches can happen. Have a plan:

- **Incident Response Team**: Assign roles for who does what in a breach scenario.

- **Notifications**: Know your legal obligations for informing customers or authorities.

- **Damage Control**: Quickly identifying how the breach occurred and what data was compromised can prevent further harm and rebuild trust more effectively.

Safeguarding Innovation at 365 Strategies

Back at 365 Strategies, Alex met with the legal team, the security group, and the department heads to discuss the sensitive AI pilot. The legal folks stressed the need for explicit client consent. Security experts insisted on encryption and limited access for employees. The conversation turned to bias as well; the data might favor certain client profiles, skewing suggestions in ways that could be seen as unfair.

"Well, if we limit ourselves to anonymized data, will we lose the personal touch that makes our proposals so appealing?" one department lead asked.

Alex nodded, acknowledging the trade-off. "That's why we'll weigh the benefits of personalization against the risks. Maybe we use partial anonymization—strip out certain personally identifiable details, but still allow broad trends to come through. And we'll set up a review process, so if the AI suggests something questionable, a human can step in and evaluate before it's implemented."

Jordan listened quietly, then spoke up. "Let's proceed, but only if we have a firm plan: how we get consent, how we handle the data, and how we explain this to clients."

In the following weeks, Alex rolled out a privacy checklist for new AI projects: verify data sources, confirm compliance with local laws, apply anonymization if feasible, and engage an internal review board whenever an initiative had potential ethical pitfalls. It wasn't a simple or quick process, but it calmed nerves across the company. Employees felt more secure knowing there were guidelines in place, and clients appreciated that 365 Strategies wasn't just recklessly diving into AI without considering the repercussions.

Reflecting on the journey, Alex realized that protecting security, privacy, and ethics wasn't a secondary concern—it was core to making AI work for everyone. Without these guardrails, even the most impressive AI tool could backfire, damaging reputations and trust. By thoughtfully addressing each of these dimensions, 365 Strategies wasn't just coding a model; it was building a sustainable future where innovation and responsibility went hand in hand.

PART III: INTRODUCING THE GAIN MODEL

OVERVIEW OF THE GAIN MODEL

A Lightbulb Moment at the Conference

Alex shifted in their seat, balancing a notepad and coffee cup, while a lively keynote speaker paced across the stage at an industry conference. The speaker was talking about a framework called "GAIN," which stood for Ground Floor, Advance, Innovate, and New Horizons—a structured way to chart an organization's path through AI adoption. The more Alex listened, the more they felt an almost electrifying sense of clarity.

Scribbling frantic notes, Alex realized this model might be exactly what 365 Strategies needed. At the office, there had been countless discussions about which AI project to tackle first or how to move from small pilots to bigger transformations. But the conversations often felt disjointed, with each department championing its own agenda. The GAIN model laid out a clear progression, showing that AI adoption could be methodical rather than haphazard.

Once the speaker wrapped up, Alex hurried to the conference lobby, excitedly flipping through notes and jotting down ideas on how to adapt GAIN for 365 Strategies. "Finally," Alex thought, "I have a framework that explains how to move from basic automation all the way to truly game-changing AI innovations." Over the next few days, Alex couldn't wait to share this discovery back at the office, envisioning how GAIN could bring everyone onto the same page.

Understanding the GAIN Model

The GAIN model outlines four stages of AI maturity: Ground Floor, Advance, Innovate, and New Horizons. Each stage represents a deeper level of AI integration and impact within an organization. By understanding these stages, leaders and teams can recognize where they currently stand and plan where they'd like to go next.

1. Ground Floor—Laying the Foundation

- **Definition**: At the Ground Floor stage, AI is introduced in simple, low-risk ways. Organizations typically use AI to replicate tasks that humans already do, often to reduce manual work or speed up routine processes.

- **Examples**: Automating data entry, converting paperwork into digital forms, or using rule-based chatbots for basic customer inquiries.

- **Key Benefits**:

  - *Quick Wins*: Visible efficiency improvements help build confidence.

  - *Team Buy-In*: Employees see immediate relief from repetitive tasks and grow more open to AI's potential.

- **Challenges**: Organizations can get stuck here if they never move beyond superficial automations. The focus on simple tasks may overshadow bigger AI opportunities.

2. Advance—Enhancing Existing Processes

- **Definition**: In the Advance stage, AI doesn't just replace human tasks; it supercharges them. Teams use AI to accelerate existing workflows, adding speed, accuracy, or fresh insights.

- **Examples**: Predictive scheduling tools that forecast staffing needs, NLP-based chatbots that handle more complex queries, or quality control systems that spot manufacturing defects more accurately than humans.

- **Key Benefits**:

  - *Improved Performance*: AI tools deliver faster turnaround times and fewer errors.

- o *Data-Driven Insights*: Teams glean deeper patterns from data, guiding smarter decisions.

- **Challenges**: While tasks are more efficient, the underlying process is still recognizable. The organization hasn't yet reinvented how it works; it's just boosting what's already there.

3. Innovate—Transforming How Work Gets Done

- **Definition**: The Innovate stage is where AI truly reshapes existing methods. Instead of merely optimizing current processes, AI drives entirely new workflows or solutions.

- **Examples**: AI might design new products, generate fresh business models, or handle real-time analytics that radically change decision-making on the fly.

- **Key Benefits**:

  - o *Significant Competitive Edge*: Companies can differentiate themselves by offering capabilities others haven't caught up to yet.

  - o *Cultural Shift*: Employees begin expecting change and may actively look for ways AI can solve problems.

- **Challenges**: Transforming processes requires buy-in across departments. Resistance to change, lack of AI fluency, and major investments can slow progress.

4. New Horizons—Reinventing the Business Model

- **Definition**: In this final stage, AI isn't just a tool; it's a platform for wholly new possibilities. Organizations launch products, services, or revenue streams that would be impossible without AI at the core.

- **Examples**: Companies introducing personalized, AI-driven offerings, city-scale analytics platforms for public services, or entirely new markets based on AI insights.

- **Key Benefits**:

    o *Industry Leadership*: By pioneering fresh business models, these organizations often become trendsetters.

    o *Scalable Value*: AI evolves alongside the business, continually opening up novel opportunities.

- **Challenges**: Maintaining ethical and secure practices at scale can be complex. The pace of innovation might outstrip existing policies, demanding robust frameworks to navigate new ground.

Why the GAIN Model Matters

- **Structured Progression**: GAIN ensures that organizations don't jump straight into advanced AI without first establishing a stable foundation.

- **Unified Language**: Leaders, IT teams, and stakeholders can use the same terms—Ground Floor, Advance, Innovate, New Horizons—to describe where they are and what's next.

- **Roadmap for Growth**: By identifying the current stage, a company can set realistic goals for the next milestone. This clarity guides budget decisions, training plans, and technology investments.

Introducing GAIN at 365 Strategies

Armed with the GAIN model, Alex returned to 365 Strategies and scheduled a short presentation, inviting department heads and key decision-makers. Standing at the front of the room, Alex explained how each phase allowed an organization to deepen its relationship with AI.

- "We're at the Ground Floor in some areas," Alex noted, pointing to a slide about automated data entry. "It's an improvement, but we might be missing the chance to really use AI to learn from our data."

- The next slide showed the Advance stage: "This is where AI speeds up and sharpens our existing processes—like using analytics to optimize scheduling or proposals. We have pieces of that, but it isn't widely adopted yet."

- Discussing Innovate, Alex's eyes lit up. "Here's where we'd shake up how we manage projects altogether. Maybe we'd design workflows that respond in real time to client changes, with AI guiding the adjustments. It's a bigger leap, but the payoff could be massive."

- Finally, Alex introduced New Horizons: "Imagine offering entirely new AI-driven services to our clients—maybe a subscription tool that analyzes their market trends in real time. That's beyond improving ourselves; it's creating fresh revenue streams."

A few attendees furrowed their brows, worried about the resource and cultural changes needed for Innovate or New Horizons. But others seemed excited by the possibility of leading the industry rather than following. Jordan, who had been quietly listening, asked the critical question: "So, how do we decide which stage to move to first?"

"That's the beauty of it," Alex replied. "The model encourages us to assess our capabilities and see what's realistic. Maybe we do a quick gap analysis: which processes are still manual, which can be made more efficient, and how prepared are we for bigger steps?"

The meeting ended on a high note, with several department heads voicing enthusiasm for a roadmap that felt both clear and aspirational. In the weeks that followed, Alex helped staff map their current AI projects to the stages of GAIN. By speaking the same language, the company could debate proposals more constructively, ensuring that each new AI initiative didn't just pop up haphazardly but followed a logical path toward deeper innovation.

Stepping out of the conference room, Alex felt a sense of relief. The GAIN model offered a guiding framework that simplified conversations, set shared expectations, and ensured that everyone understood AI as a journey rather than a one-time project. Armed with this model, 365 Strategies was better poised to move from basic automation to advanced transformation—one deliberate step at a time.

G (GROUND FLOOR)-LAYING THE FOUNDATION

A Simple but Surprising Start

Balancing a stack of client proposals in one arm, Alex pushed open the door to a cramped storage room at 365 Strategies. The place was packed with filing cabinets and boxes of printed documents—each one representing days, if not weeks, of manual labor. "If only we could automate half of this," Alex thought, eyeing a box labeled "Archived Proposals (2019)."

A meeting with Finance the previous day had set the wheels in motion. The team had complained about the sheer volume of paperwork involved in drafting and revising proposals. Jordan, ever on the lookout for operational efficiency, turned to Alex with a lightbulb idea: "Isn't this exactly the kind of repetitive task we could hand off to an AI or automated system? Maybe we can free our staff from the drudgery of manual data entry and formatting."

Though the concept sounded straightforward—automate mundane tasks with AI—it felt like a major leap for 365 Strategies. They'd never fully integrated an AI tool before, especially not one that handled client-facing documents. But the possibility was too tempting to ignore. If they pulled it off, staff could reclaim hours previously lost to routine tasks, leaving more time for creative thinking and client interaction. "Let's give it a shot," Jordan had said, and Alex couldn't help but feel both nervous and excited.

What Ground Floor AI Really Means

In the GAIN model, "Ground Floor" refers to the earliest stage of AI adoption—where an organization begins using AI to automate tasks that humans already perform manually. While these tasks might seem small, they're actually the critical first step in building trust, familiarity, and momentum for more advanced AI projects down the road.

1. Identifying Repetitive Tasks

The hallmark of Ground Floor AI initiatives is simplicity. Think of things like data entry, invoice processing, or converting physical documents into digital records. Because they're repetitive and follow clear rules, these tasks lend themselves well to basic automation:

- **Invoice Processing**: Software that matches line items to purchase orders, reducing errors and speeds up approvals.

- **Email Sorting or Routing**: An AI-powered system that recognizes keywords or patterns, directing messages to the right person.

- **Form Digitization**: Converting paper forms into digital data sets, saving time and storage space.

These "quick wins" prove to employees that AI can be a reliable ally in tackling day-to-day drudgery.

2. Building Confidence and Internal Buy-In

One of the biggest benefits of the Ground Floor stage is intangible: **confidence**. When employees see an AI tool handling simple tasks correctly, they become less fearful and more open to exploring AI's broader possibilities. Key outcomes include:

- **Trust**: As staff experiences fewer errors and less tedium, they start trusting technology more.

- **Skill Development**: People learn to interact with AI systems— like scanning documents or training a simple machine-learning model to recognize standard templates.

- **Culture Shift**: AI conversations become more positive as employees realize automation doesn't necessarily replace them; it empowers them to focus on higher-level tasks.

3. Scalability Without Heavy Complexity

At this stage, organizations generally don't require advanced data science teams or elaborate infrastructures. Off-the-shelf software often suffices. However, it's wise to keep track of performance data—like how much time is saved or how many errors are reduced. These metrics build the case for future AI investments.

- **Minimal Resources**: Cloud-based solutions or simple RPA (Robotic Process Automation) tools can be enough to launch a Ground Floor project.

- **Easy Maintenance**: Since these tasks don't usually change dramatically, models or automations need fewer updates.

- **Clear ROI**: When a pilot goes well, you can present cost savings or efficiency gains to leadership, paving the way for bigger projects.

4. Avoiding Pitfalls

As straightforward as Ground Floor AI can be, a few pitfalls remain:

- **Over-Promising**: Just because a task is simple doesn't mean it's easy to automate. Confirm data formats, existing workflows, and staff readiness before committing.

- **Ignoring Human Oversight**: Initially, keep humans in the loop. Even automated systems can make mistakes, especially if they encounter cases they weren't trained for.

- **Underestimating Change Management**: If employees fear automation will take away their jobs, a well-communicated rollout is crucial to ease concerns and highlight the benefits.

By taking these precautions, you ensure your AI pilot project fosters enthusiasm rather than resistance.

A Small Win with Big Impact

After weeks of collaboration between Finance, IT, and the operations team, Alex finally launched the new automated system that handled routine client proposals. It wasn't the flashiest AI tool on the market, but it worked: staff would upload a standard proposal template, and the system would populate the main fields by pulling data from a centralized repository. Simple checks guaranteed that the correct client name, project dates, and pricing details were included.

The result? Hours once spent on repetitive data entry were now freed up. Finance could focus on double-checking the more critical parts of each proposal instead of getting bogged down in basic formatting. Even the marketing team, which often provided last-minute edits, found they could refine content faster. "I had no idea how much time we were wasting on mindless copying and pasting," one team member admitted.

Encouraged by this success, Alex noticed a ripple effect. People started casually asking, "What else can AI handle?" or "Could we automate that, too?" The small, contained victory gave everyone a taste of AI's potential without overwhelming them with complex data science jargon.

During a meeting to review initial results, Jordan nodded approvingly. "This is just the beginning. If automating basic tasks can save us this much time and energy, imagine what we can achieve if we move further up the GAIN model."

For Alex, it was a moment of validation. The Ground Floor stage didn't involve flashy breakthroughs or sophisticated machine learning algorithms—but it proved that AI, even in its simplest form, could spark a tangible shift in how people viewed technology and its place at 365 Strategies. The door was now open for bigger, bolder initiatives. And with that momentum, Alex felt ready to explore the next step of the GAIN journey—knowing the foundation was solidly in place.

A (ADVANCE)-IMPROVING EFFICIENCY AND ACCURACY

Stepping Beyond Simple Automation

Not long after rolling out a successful AI pilot to automate routine proposals, Alex found themselves fielding a new wave of questions at 365 Strategies. "What else can AI do?" colleagues would ask. "Could we use it to forecast project timelines or spot hidden cost overruns?" This growing curiosity signaled that the company was ready for the Advance stage of the GAIN model—where AI becomes more than a timesaver and starts truly enhancing existing workflows.

A meeting with Jordan and the operations team pinpointed a pressing issue: scheduling. The firm often grappled with project bottlenecks, either understaffing crucial tasks or over-allocating people who then sat idle. "If we had a predictive tool," Jordan mused, "it could analyze patterns in past projects and help us allocate our staff more effectively."

Alex couldn't help but nod in excitement. It was the perfect challenge for the Advance phase. The workflow—staff assigning people to projects—would stay the same on the surface, but an AI-driven scheduling tool could reduce friction and guesswork. Imagine the system scanning upcoming deadlines, team availability, and project complexities, then recommending optimal staffing plans. No one was talking about removing human managers from the loop, but the right data-driven insights could drastically cut down on last-minute scrambles.

Elevating Workflows in the Advance Stage

In the GAIN model, moving from Ground Floor to Advance means shifting from basic automation to more purposeful AI that refines how tasks are done—without yet overhauling the entire process. The system might look the same to an outsider, but behind the scenes, AI adds speed, accuracy, and richer insights.

1. Using AI to Enhance, Not Replace

At the Advance stage, AI amplifies human judgment rather than eliminating it. People still guide the system, but they rely on algorithmic insights for speed and precision. For example:

- **Predictive Analytics**: Tools that anticipate outcomes—like forecasting sales, predicting maintenance needs, or staffing demands.

- **Smart Recommendations**: Systems that suggest next steps for employees, whether it's recommending additional training or prioritizing tasks based on deadlines.

Think of it as an assistant that helps employees do their jobs more efficiently, instead of fully automating those roles. By offering a "second opinion" or an extra layer of analysis, AI enables humans to focus on tasks where critical thinking and creativity shine.

2. Spotlight on Accuracy and Efficiency

One of the biggest gains in this stage is reducing errors. While basic automation might prevent typos in data entry, advanced AI can do things like:

- **Spot Anomalies**: If numbers suddenly spike in a project budget, an AI tool can flag this for review.

- **Minimize Scheduling Conflicts**: AI can cross-reference vacation calendars, client deadlines, and resource availability to provide more accurate timetables.

- **Optimize Production**: In manufacturing or service industries, AI can optimize processes to minimize downtime, scrap rates, or shipping delays.

The upshot is better resource use, leading to cost savings and fewer bottlenecks. Everyone still does their jobs, but the friction disappears.

3. Data Insights You Didn't Know You Had

Another hallmark of the Advance stage is deeper data mining. While Ground Floor solutions might just replicate tasks humans do manually, advanced AI systems dig into historical records to unearth patterns. This often requires:

- **Clean, Consolidated Data**: Ensuring your data pipeline is robust, so the AI has quality data to learn from.

- **Cross-Functional Input**: People from various departments share different types of data, making the system's recommendations more holistic.

- **Iterative Improvement**: The AI learns from new data, improving recommendations over time.

By systematically analyzing the "lessons" from past activities, teams spot trends that no single person would have time to unravel manually—like the unexpected correlation between certain team combinations and project success rates.

4. Managing Expectations

While the Advance stage promises significant gains, it's important to set realistic goals:

- **AI Isn't Magic**: Staff need to know that while AI reduces guesswork, it doesn't guarantee perfect predictions.

- **Pilot and Refine**: Launching in a single department (e.g., operations scheduling) before scaling to the entire company can catch issues early.

- **Ongoing Training**: Team members should understand how to interpret AI outputs. If the system flags a scheduling conflict, people need to know why and what to do next.

Clear communication about AI's role prevents disillusionment if results aren't immediate or if the tool occasionally produces odd suggestions.

A Productivity Booster at 365 Strategies

With leadership's blessing, Alex assembled a small cross-functional team—operations managers, data specialists, and an IT liaison—to pilot a new scheduling tool. They fed the system information from past projects: durations, required skills, bottlenecks, and actual versus planned staffing. Over a few weeks, the AI began to predict which tasks would require the most personnel, which parts of a project were likely to drag behind schedule, and which employees had relevant experience.

When the first set of recommendations arrived, the ops managers were a bit skeptical. "It suggests putting Tanya on two overlapping projects?" one asked. But the tool had recognized Tanya's skill overlap and predicted she could handle the front-end tasks of one project before seamlessly switching to a later phase of another. Over the course of a month, managers realized the tool's suggestions often made sense— enough that they began to trust it for routine scheduling. They still applied their own judgment, especially when dealing with unexpected client requests or personal constraints, but the AI cut down on the guesswork.

Before long, the results were visible. Projects ran more smoothly, with fewer panic moments from staff shortages or underused employees. The difference wasn't revolutionary—operations still looked the same from a bird's-eye view. But deeper down, the tool was orchestrating staffing decisions with newfound precision. Team members marveled at how data-driven planning left them more time to tackle pressing client issues and creative problem-solving, instead of scrambling to fill resource gaps at the last minute.

In a wrap-up meeting, Jordan praised the scheduling pilot. "We're saving hours of back-and-forth. People see how the AI suggestions pan out, and the confidence in the tool grows each week." The success opened discussions about applying similar predictive analytics to other areas—maybe financial forecasting or client proposal timelines.

For Alex, this was a turning point. The Ground Floor stage had introduced AI as a reliable helper, but at the Advance stage, it became clear that AI could do much more than handle busywork. It could reshape how an existing workflow operated, boosting efficiency and sharpening accuracy, without overturning the whole process. And with that, the 365 Strategies team began to realize how AI, applied wisely, could lift them beyond the basics—pointing toward even more transformative opportunities on the horizon.

I (INNOVATE)-REDESIGNING PROCESSES AND METHODS

A Bold New Proposal

After months of steady progress automating tasks and optimizing workflows with AI, Alex sat in a brainstorming session at 365 Strategies, feeling a familiar nudge of excitement. The meeting started with a simple question: "What if we used AI to completely reimagine how we write client proposals?" The query came from a senior consultant who'd noticed that, despite new tools for scheduling and analytics, the actual content creation process still ate up hours of staff time.

Alex couldn't help but recall the early days, when the team's focus was on smaller wins—automating data entry, smoothing out scheduling. But now, 365 Strategies seemed ready for something bigger, something that transcended minor efficiency gains. Maybe a generative AI system could analyze past proposals, incorporate current client data, and generate initial drafts that consultants could refine. It sounded both ambitious and a bit unnerving: Would AI produce content that felt authentic? Could it truly reflect each client's unique challenges?

Yet the more Alex envisioned the idea, the more it fit into the Innovate stage of the GAIN model. This wasn't just speeding up a process; it was changing how the entire company might approach proposal writing. It could free staff from repetitive drafting and allow them to spend time on strategic thinking. Sipping coffee and scribbling notes, Alex resolved to pitch a pilot project at the next leadership meeting—even if it meant challenging the comfort zone of some coworkers.

Embracing the Innovate Stage

In the GAIN framework, Innovate represents the moment AI shifts from enhancing existing processes to fundamentally redesigning them. This level of adoption often involves experimentation with generative

AI, real-time data dashboards, or other capabilities that make people rethink their usual methods. Although it can feel like a big leap, it's a natural evolution if an organization has already built trust in AI through more incremental projects.

1. Moving Beyond Incremental Improvements

Whereas the previous stages (Ground Floor and Advance) focus on efficiency and reliability, Innovate seeks to create new possibilities. AI isn't just a tool that speeds things up; it becomes a collaborative partner that shapes how tasks are conceived and executed. This can manifest in several ways:

- **Generative AI Tools**: Systems that not only analyze data but also produce creative outputs—like drafting text, designing prototypes, or generating product concepts.

- **Real-Time, Data-Driven Decision-Making**: Dashboards that continuously update with streaming data, allowing teams to pivot strategies on the fly rather than waiting for monthly reports.

- **Cross-Functional Experimentation**: AI ideas no longer sit in one department. Multiple teams collaborate, leading to hybrid solutions that didn't exist before.

The result is often a culture of rapid testing and learning, where staff can prototype bold ideas quickly, evaluate feedback, and iterate without fear.

2. Overcoming Resistance to New Methods

Innovation can be uncomfortable. Teams used to certain workflows might find the introduction of radically different processes jarring or risky:

- **Fear of Replacing Expertise**: Employees may worry an AI-driven approach will overshadow their creativity or diminish their professional value.

- **Technical Uncertainty**: Deploying more advanced AI (like generative models) may demand specialized expertise or infrastructure upgrades, leading to hesitation.

- **Skepticism About Quality**: Colleagues may question whether AI outputs are accurate or culturally appropriate.

These concerns can be addressed with open communication, incremental rollouts, and a clear demonstration of how AI complements rather than replaces human skills.

3. The Collaborative Human-AI Model

One misconception about innovating with AI is that machines will do everything. In reality, the most powerful innovations often pair AI's computational speed with human intuition. For instance:

- **Initial Drafting**: An AI tool might compile data, statistics, and common language from prior documents to draft a proposal. But humans refine tone, style, and strategy.

- **Real-Time Analytics**: A dashboard can present trends, but humans decide what those trends mean in context.

- **Creative Ideation**: Some AI systems generate product sketches or marketing angles, while humans blend them with real-world constraints and brand identity.

In short, AI acts as a creative catalyst, freeing up humans to engage in higher-level thinking, ethical judgments, and empathetic communication—areas where machines still lag.

4. Measuring Success in the Innovate Stage

When processes are redesigned, traditional metrics like cost savings or time reduction might not capture the full impact. Leaders often look at:

- **Quality of Outcomes**: Does the new method produce better results, higher sales, or more successful client pitches?

- **Employee Engagement**: Are people more energized by their roles now that mundane tasks are minimized and creative thinking is emphasized?

- **Speed of Adaptation**: How quickly can teams respond to unexpected changes or client requests?

- **New Opportunities**: Has the innovation led to fresh service lines or products that didn't exist before?

By tracking these broader measures, organizations see not just incremental improvements but genuine transformation.

A Whole New Way to Craft Proposals

At the leadership meeting, Alex braced for mixed reactions while outlining the plan: an AI tool would gather data from past successful proposals, client reports, and even relevant market research. With a few parameters specified (like client industry and desired scope), the system would generate a draft proposal. Human consultants would then refine it for clarity, persuasion, and that personal touch clients expect.

Some colleagues raised eyebrows: "Won't clients notice an AI wrote part of the proposal?" Others questioned the reliability of such drafts. But as Alex explained, the goal wasn't to remove human insight; it was to let AI handle repetitive baseline content, references, and structure. Consultants would retain control, shaping the final product with their expertise and client relationships.

Jordan leaned forward. "We could pilot this on a small set of clients who already trust us," he suggested. "If it bombs, we revert to our usual process. If it works, we could see a big drop in proposal turnaround time and possibly better alignment with client goals." The room buzzed with cautious excitement.

A few weeks later, the pilot launched. The AI-generated drafts weren't perfect—some sections needed heavy edits. But overall, the system pulled together relevant case studies, compliance details, and updated pricing models far more quickly than a human could. For the first time, the proposal team found themselves focusing on high-level narratives and strategic angles rather than hunting for basic data. "It's like having an intern who's super-fast at research but still needs you to make sense of everything," one consultant joked.

Soon, the results spoke for themselves. Proposal creation time dropped significantly, and clients noticed the extra customization and thought that the final documents displayed. Instead of reusing old templates with minor tweaks, teams had more energy to tailor each proposal's vision. Enthusiasm spread as departments realized AI could genuinely liberate them from certain mechanical tasks, allowing them to innovate not just how they worked, but how they collaborated and ideated.

Alex knew this shift marked a major milestone in 365 Strategies' AI journey. The Innovate stage wasn't just about adopting another tool; it was about rethinking the entire proposal process, empowering consultants to be more strategic and creative. It felt risky at first—like stepping off a well-worn path into uncharted territory—but the payoff was clear: when AI and human expertise combined at this deeper level, the firm could offer clients something new, something that transcended the old boundaries of what a consulting firm could deliver.

N (NEW HORIZONS)-PIONEERING FRESH OPPORTUNITIES

Envisioning a Bold Future

After witnessing AI transform how proposals were written and schedules were managed, Alex felt a growing sense that 365 Strategies was ready for more than just incremental or even innovative changes. One evening, while reviewing a handful of AI success stories from other industries, an idea took shape: What if 365 Strategies built its own AI-based platform to offer clients on a subscription basis?

It was a radical thought. For years, the firm's bread and butter had been consulting—diagnosing problems, presenting solutions, and guiding implementation. A platform, however, would make AI-driven insights available to clients 24/7, without requiring a full consulting engagement each time. It could scan market data, generate real-time recommendations, and even learn from ongoing client usage to personalize advice.

Scribbling furiously in a notebook, Alex drafted a rough sketch of this subscription model: potential features, target pricing, and how it might scale. Sure, it would require significant development and a dedicated support team, but it also opened up entirely new revenue possibilities. This vision fit perfectly with the final stage of the GAIN model—New Horizons—where AI-driven capabilities push an organization into uncharted territory, potentially redefining its entire business model.

Embracing the New Horizons Stage

In the GAIN framework, New Horizons represents the apex of AI adoption. At this level, organizations are no longer just automating tasks or enhancing existing processes; they're pioneering ideas, products, or services that couldn't have existed without AI's transformative capabilities.

1. Beyond Improvement to Reinvention

By the time a company reaches New Horizons, AI is deeply woven into its DNA. Rather than merely optimizing existing workflows, leadership now asks, "What can we create that never existed before?" This could mean:

- **Launching AI-Based Products**: Tools or platforms that clients can use directly, rather than just consulting solutions.

- **Entering New Markets**: Using AI insights to pivot into industries or customer segments the organization hasn't served before.

- **Radical Redesign of Value Propositions**: Offering subscription models, predictive services, or personalized experiences that set the organization apart from competitors.

It's not just about doing the old work better; it's about reimagining what the company can deliver to the world.

2. High Risk, High Reward

This final stage is exciting but also risky. Venturing into new territory without the usual safety nets can be daunting. Challenges often include:

- **Significant Investment**: Building robust AI products requires specialized talent, potentially from data scientists to software engineers, plus dedicated infrastructure for real-time analytics.

- **Cultural Shift**: Staff must adapt to the idea of being a product company (or a platform provider), not just a consulting service or traditional business.

- **Complex Compliance and Liability**: When you offer an AI-driven service externally, you carry responsibility for data security, ethical use, and ongoing performance.

Despite these hurdles, New Horizons can catapult an organization to industry leadership—if it's prepared to manage the uncertainties.

3. Partnership and Ecosystem Strategies

At this stage, many companies find that collaborating with other organizations—startups, universities, or even competitors—can accelerate their AI journey. Partnerships might offer:

- **Technical Expertise**: If you lack in-house machine learning engineers or UX designers, a strategic alliance can fill those gaps.

- **Shared Data**: Pooling data across partners can lead to richer insights and more effective AI models.

- **Co-Marketing Opportunities**: Launching an AI platform with a trusted partner can expand your market reach and credibility.

By forging these alliances, organizations can offset some of the cost and complexity that come with developing brand-new AI-driven solutions.

4. Measuring Impact at New Horizons

Traditional ROI metrics—like reduced operational costs—may no longer capture the full value of an AI-driven product or service. Leaders often track:

- **Recurring Revenue**: How many clients subscribe to the new platform or service?

- **Market Share**: Does this AI-enabled offering help the company enter untapped markets or outpace competitors?

- **Strategic Influence**: Has the company's brand evolved, influencing industry standards or drawing partnerships?

- **Long-Term Innovation Pipeline**: Is the new platform serving as a launchpad for further experimentation and AI-based features?

The central theme is that AI is no longer a support function but a **core generator** of new business opportunities.

Elevating 365 Strategies to a New Frontier

With the rough sketch of an AI-driven subscription platform in hand, Alex approached Jordan and the senior leadership team. Nerves fluttered, but excitement prevailed. "We have this wealth of data—client projects, industry benchmarks, predictive models we've already built. Why not package that into a tool clients can access anytime? We'd be transitioning from a project-based model to a subscription-based one. Yes, it's a leap, but it could be a game-changer."

A hush fell over the conference room. Someone from Finance raised concerns about upfront costs—building a scalable, secure platform wasn't cheap. Others worried about support: would the consulting team shift roles to become product managers and customer success reps? But the potential was undeniable. Imagine if 365 Strategies could provide clients with real-time strategy insights, project scheduling forecasts, and even competitor analysis through one unified AI hub.

Gradually, the discussion turned from if to how. They decided to start small with a beta version for a handful of long-standing clients who trusted 365 Strategies and had expressed frustration with standard consulting timelines. Alex led a cross-departmental task force: IT would handle the infrastructure, data scientists would refine the AI models, and consultants would shape the platform's user interface and content. The project timeline was ambitious, but morale was high.

Within a few months, the first clients gained access. They could log in, view predictive market reports, and even generate initial strategy outlines. The reaction was overwhelmingly positive. "It's like having a mini-consultant available around the clock," one client said, "but it still feels like it has 365 Strategies' expertise behind it."

That blend of AI efficiency and human-backed expertise epitomized New Horizons—an offering that simply didn't exist before advanced AI made it possible. For Alex, the moment felt triumphant. The journey from basic automation to launching an AI-centric product was anything but easy. Yet here they were, forging a path where AI would no longer be a behind-the-scenes tool but a centerpiece of the company's identity.

In the grander scheme, 365 Strategies' leap to New Horizons didn't just mean more revenue. It meant the firm was evolving into something greater than it had ever been—an organization that didn't just follow industry trends but helped define them. And that, ultimately, was the power of a well-executed AI strategy: to unlock horizons that previously seemed out of reach, propelling the entire company forward into a future with limitless possibilities.

PART IV: DRIVING AI SUCCESS IN PRACTICE

BEST PRACTICES IN AI PROJECT MANAGEMENT

Balancing Multiple Pilots

One gray Monday morning, Alex opened the project dashboard and blinked at the sheer number of AI initiatives happening at 365 Strategies. There was the predictive scheduling tool for Operations, the new generative AI engine for proposals, and an ambitious pilot in Finance aimed at automating invoice reviews. Each project had its own timeline, budget, and set of stakeholders—some more vocal than others.

In the past, Alex had overseen typical consulting engagements with relatively predictable milestones. But AI projects felt different. Models needed regular retraining, data pipelines required constant upkeep, and users had to give feedback on prototypes before too much development time was sunk in the wrong direction. Even small changes in data quality could cause a chain reaction, throwing off model results and pushing deadlines back.

Jordan, sensing Alex's tension, pulled them aside. "These AI pilots are expanding quickly," Jordan said, tapping on the project board. "We need a way to manage them effectively, or we'll burn out the team and lose momentum."

Alex nodded, aware that traditional methods of project management didn't always fit the iterative nature of AI work. It was time to lean into more flexible approaches like agile or scrum—techniques that allowed for frequent check-ins, course corrections, and collaborative input from multiple departments. If done well, these methods could balance the creative freedom needed for AI with the structure required to hit key targets.

Mastering AI Project Management

Managing AI initiatives requires a blend of classical project management skills and the adaptability to handle the evolving nature of machine learning, data engineering, and user feedback. Here's how to keep these unique projects running smoothly:

1. Embrace Agile or Scrum Methodologies

Unlike standard IT projects that can be planned out meticulously from start to finish, AI often needs more experimentation. The agile approach involves breaking work into sprints—short, focused periods (often two weeks) where the team commits to delivering specific pieces of functionality or improvements. Each sprint ends with a review session, giving stakeholders an opportunity to see progress, offer feedback, and adjust priorities.

Key Agile Practices:

- **Daily Stand-Ups**: Quick team check-ins to align on tasks, voice blockers, and coordinate efforts.

- **Sprint Reviews**: Demonstrate new features or model outputs, allowing real-time user feedback.

- **Retrospectives**: Reflect on what went well and what needs improvement, then apply lessons to the next sprint.

This iterative model ensures the AI project remains relevant to user needs, accommodates changing data conditions, and catches issues early.

2. Build in Time for Model Iterations

AI development rarely follows a linear path. Models get trained, tested, tweaked, and retrained. Data might change, requiring further adjustments. Integrating buffer time into each phase is crucial. Consider:

- **Data Exploration**: Allocating time for data scientists to explore and clean new datasets.

- **Algorithm Tuning**: Experiments with different models, parameters, or hyperparameters to boost accuracy.

- **Validation Cycles**: Repeated testing against real or simulated scenarios ensures models hold up in production.

If you schedule AI milestones too rigidly, you risk rushing model iterations, leading to subpar results and frustrated teams.

3. Engage Stakeholders Early and Often

Because AI can drastically alter workflows, it's vital that end users and department heads are involved from the outset. This not only secures buy-in but also provides valuable insights. Some best practices include:

- **Regular Demos**: Showing prototypes to potential users ensures that the tool aligns with real-world needs.

- **Cross-Functional Teams**: Having representatives from finance, operations, IT, and marketing fosters broader perspectives and anticipates potential conflicts.

- **Transparent Communication**: Discuss realistic timelines, potential risks, and the iterative nature of AI. Setting the right expectations from day one reduces misunderstandings.

4. Define Metrics for Success

AI projects can drift if they lack clear goals or measurement criteria. Agree on Key Performance Indicators (KPIs) before development begins. These might include:

- **Accuracy**: If building a predictive model, what accuracy or error margin is acceptable?

- **Time Saved**: For automation projects, measure the reduction in manual hours.

- **User Adoption**: How many people or departments actively use the new AI tool?

- **ROI**: Track financial benefits, whether through cost savings, new revenue streams, or reduced errors.

Review these KPIs at each milestone to confirm the project is on track or determine if the team needs to pivot.

5. Manage the Data Lifecycle

Data isn't static. It changes as the business evolves, which can break or degrade AI models:

- **Ongoing Data Governance**: Ensure data sources are updated, clean, and compliant with privacy regulations.

- **Version Control for Models**: Label each model version, capturing training data details and performance metrics so you can roll back if needed.

- **Continuous Monitoring**: Keep an eye on model drift—when real-world data shifts away from what the model was trained on, diminishing accuracy.

By treating data as a living asset, teams can maintain the reliability of AI solutions over time.

Finding Flow in Complexity

In the weeks following Jordan's hint toward more agile methods, Alex began structuring the multiple AI pilots into sprints. Operation scheduling, finance automation, and marketing analytics each had their own sprint boards, with tasks broken into manageable chunks. Daily stand-ups helped Alex spot potential roadblocks—like a mismatch between data formatting and the model's input requirements—before they derailed entire timelines.

Meanwhile, stakeholders quickly saw the benefit of these frequent check-ins. The finance team could request a new feature mid-sprint if they discovered an efficiency opportunity, rather than waiting until the project wrapped. The marketing group gained early glimpses of their analytics dashboard, offering feedback that saved development time down the line. While it meant more frequent communication, it also prevented misunderstandings and delivered small, tangible wins faster.

Not everything was smooth sailing. A couple of times, the AI outputs underperformed because data pipelines weren't feeding fresh information as expected. Instead of panicking, Alex and the data engineers used sprint retrospectives to identify the bottlenecks and fix them before the next cycle. The iterative rhythm of agile kept the pilots moving forward, even in the face of unpredictable changes.

Seeing how these principles brought structure to AI's inherent uncertainty, Alex felt relieved and inspired. "We can handle the complexity," they realized, "as long as we keep adapting, collecting feedback, and focusing on the metrics that matter." By applying best practices in AI project management, 365 Strategies was proving that juggling multiple pilots didn't have to be chaotic; with agile sprints, stakeholder engagement, and clear success measures, the firm could push AI forward in a steady, sustainable way.

BUILDING YOUR AI TEAM AND CULTURE

A "Boot Camp" That Sparks Excitement

After rolling out several AI initiatives at 365 Strategies, Alex noticed a new buzz in the office corridors. Some employees were eager to learn how AI tools worked behind the scenes, while others felt left out, unsure whether they had the right skills to contribute. Realizing that strong AI adoption required more than just a small group of specialists, Alex pitched an idea to Jordan: an internal AI "boot camp."

Jordan raised an eyebrow. "You want to teach data science and coding to the entire staff?"

Alex shrugged but grinned. "Not the entire staff. But I see a lot of junior associates hungry to pick up these skills. Some senior project managers, too, want to see how AI can enhance their workflows. We don't need everyone becoming an AI engineer, but we do need everyone feeling they can have a say in our AI projects."

And so, the plan took shape: a series of workshops, tutorials, and hands-on labs that would introduce AI basics to anyone curious enough to join—no advanced math degrees required. To Alex's delight, sign-ups came from all corners: finance analysts, marketing associates, project managers, and even a couple of HR coordinators. It was the perfect chance to transform AI from a specialized concept into a shared learning journey across the company.

Building a Sustainable AI Culture

A successful AI initiative extends beyond the technology itself; it's also about people and culture. Whether you're recruiting new talent or training existing staff, the goal is to foster an environment where AI knowledge is shared, curiosity is encouraged, and innovation thrives.

1. Hiring and Upskilling Strategies

When it comes to assembling an AI-capable team, organizations often face a choice:

- **Hire Specialized Talent**: Bringing on data scientists, machine learning engineers, or AI architects with deep technical backgrounds. This can accelerate advanced projects but may be expensive or competitive in the job market.

- **Upskill Existing Employees**: Offer trainings, workshops, and online courses so current staff can learn AI fundamentals. This approach might take longer, but it boosts employee morale and ensures domain expertise stays in-house.

In many cases, companies find a balance: they hire a few experts to lead complex technical efforts while upskilling employees who already understand the company's culture and business needs.

2. Creating Cross-Functional Collaboration

AI isn't just for IT or data science teams; effective projects require diverse perspectives:

- **Domain Experts**: Employees who deeply understand a business area (like finance or logistics) can guide AI developers to produce relevant, practical solutions.

- **Technical Leads**: Data scientists and machine learning engineers bring expertise in algorithms, model training, and data infrastructure.

- **Project Managers and Product Owners**: They keep initiatives on track, coordinate between stakeholders, and translate business goals into project milestones.

Forming cross-functional squads encourages knowledge exchange and prevents AI from becoming a "black box" understood by only a few.

3. Encouraging a Growth Mindset

Building an AI culture often means shifting how people view learning and experimentation:

- **Celebrate Small Wins**: Acknowledge even modest successes in AI pilots, reinforcing that exploration and iteration are part of the process.

- **Normalize Failure**: Some AI experiments won't pan out. Leaders should model an attitude of learning from mistakes rather than assigning blame.

- **Offer Continuous Training**: As tools evolve, so must skills. Regular workshops, online courses, and peer coaching keep staff engaged with the latest AI developments.

By removing fear and promoting curiosity, organizations can cultivate an environment where employees volunteer ideas and wholeheartedly engage in AI projects.

4. Avoiding an "AI Elite"

It's tempting to gather a small group of AI experts and isolate them from the rest of the company. But this can hinder broad adoption and create bottlenecks:

- **Transparent Communication**: Regularly update the entire company on AI initiatives. Share success stories, lessons learned, and new goals.

- **Knowledge Sharing**: Encourage your experts to mentor others, host internal webinars, and document processes.

- **Inclusive Decision-Making**: Let non-technical voices shape AI priorities. Sometimes a frontline employee sees a pain point that leadership overlooks.

When AI is understood and championed across all levels, projects gain wider support and higher chances of success.

The Transformation from Within

The internal AI "boot camp" Alex launched felt more like a vibrant community event than a sterile training program. Junior associates giggled as they wrote their first lines of Python to analyze basic datasets. Senior project managers, initially hesitant, began brainstorming how AI-generated insights could streamline client deliverables. An unexpected camaraderie flourished, bridging gaps between departments that rarely collaborated.

Alex organized weekly "demo days" where participants shared mini-projects or discoveries. One team used a free machine-learning library to predict which sales leads were most likely to convert. Another explored text analysis on client feedback, spotting recurring themes that could guide product improvements. The excitement spilled over into everyday work, with employees eager to spot more places AI could help.

Of course, not everyone became a technical whiz. But even those who didn't dive into coding walked away with a stronger grasp of AI's fundamentals and possibilities. The biggest shift, Alex realized, was cultural: people no longer viewed AI as an arcane specialty. They saw it as an evolving tool—one that could help them solve real problems and innovate.

Jordan noticed the buzz, too. "It's amazing how much talent we had right under our noses," he said at a leadership meeting. "They just needed the chance and support to learn." Suddenly, AI adoption became less about top-down mandates and more about ground-level enthusiasm and grassroots projects.

Reflecting on the journey, Alex felt proud that 365 Strategies had taken AI beyond the IT department. By nurturing a learning culture, the firm was steadily reducing silos, boosting morale, and laying the groundwork for AI-driven success across every level of the organization.

MEASURING AI SUCCESS—ROI, KPIS, AND BEYOND

Proving the Value at 365 Strategies

Late on a Friday afternoon, Alex found themselves hunched over a makeshift spreadsheet listing out every AI project at 365 Strategies—alongside their initial cost, estimated time savings, and any feedback from staff or clients. Jordan had requested a progress report for the executive team, and Alex knew that numbers alone wouldn't cut it. Yes, the finance-driven stakeholders cared about ROI, but others wanted to hear about how AI was affecting morale and whether clients viewed the firm more favorably.

As Alex clicked through different data points—like how long it used to take to draft a basic proposal versus how quickly the AI-driven system handled the initial stage—two questions kept surfacing: "Are these projects truly delivering the promised returns?" and "How do we measure benefits that don't fit neatly into a spreadsheet?"

Over the next few days, Alex began reaching out to project leads, collecting anecdotes on how the new scheduling tool had improved staff quality of life, and checking client satisfaction metrics after they'd interacted with the AI proposal system. It quickly became clear that "success" in AI projects was about much more than just dollars and cents. In a firm as multifaceted as 365 Strategies, capturing the broader effects—like boosted team morale or a reputation for cutting-edge work—could be just as crucial for future growth.

Balancing Tangible and Intangible Metrics

Measuring the success of AI isn't a one-dimensional task. While financial metrics often grab the spotlight, it's important to go beyond mere dollars saved or earned. A holistic approach to measurement ensures that an organization captures the full scope of AI's impact—both the direct returns and the broader cultural or brand-related outcomes.

1. Traditional ROI and Cost-Benefit Analysis

For many stakeholders, the first question about AI is, "How does it affect the bottom line?" Financial metrics still matter:

- **Reduced Labor Costs**: If an AI tool automates tasks that once took hundreds of manual hours, you can calculate the cost savings.

- **Efficiency Gains**: Quantify improvements in production or service speed. Fewer backlogs mean more revenue opportunities or better client satisfaction.

- **Revenue Uplift**: Has the AI-driven service uncovered new leads or closed deals faster?

These figures are often easier to grasp, especially for finance teams. Solid ROI calculations can justify further investments in AI or help prioritize which initiatives to scale.

2. Key Performance Indicators (KPIs) for AI Projects

While ROI is a valuable anchor, additional KPIs can help paint a complete picture:

- **Accuracy or Error Rate**: For predictive models or automation tasks, track how accurately the AI performs compared to previous methods.

- **Throughput**: Measure if AI helps the team handle more projects or clients simultaneously without increasing headcount.

- **User Adoption**: A sophisticated model is worthless if no one uses it. Monitor how many employees or clients regularly engage with the AI tool.

- **Client Satisfaction**: Did customer feedback improve after introducing AI-driven insights or faster service? Customer retention or Net Promoter Scores might also reflect these changes.

Selecting the right KPIs depends on the nature of each AI initiative, but they all help pinpoint where the technology is delivering value—or falling short.

3. Intangible Benefits: Morale, Brand Perception, and More

Not every advantage of AI shows up on a balance sheet:

- **Employee Morale**: Automating tedious tasks can boost job satisfaction, leading to lower turnover or higher engagement. Ask teams how they feel about their evolving roles.

- **Brand Reputation**: Offering AI-driven solutions can position the company as innovative. Keep an eye on media mentions, social media buzz, or feedback from prospective clients.

- **Learning Culture**: AI adoption might encourage employees to learn new skills or collaborate across departments, generating an atmosphere of continuous improvement.

These less quantifiable benefits can still inform strategic decisions. For instance, if AI upgrades are attracting more job candidates or winning new clients who admire tech-savvy firms, that's a sign of indirect success.

4. Collecting and Presenting the Data

- **Survey Methods**: Gather employee and client feedback through short polls or interviews. Include questions about AI tools, general satisfaction, or perceived productivity gains.

- **Dashboards**: Build a centralized dashboard tracking both numeric metrics (like cost savings) and softer measures (like user satisfaction). This keeps stakeholders informed at a glance.

- **Regular Review Sessions**: Schedule periodic check-ins with leadership to discuss whether AI projects are hitting targets. Use these meetings to refine KPIs if the initial ones don't fully capture progress.

By blending objective metrics with qualitative insights, managers can steer AI projects in the right direction while maintaining buy-in from everyone.

5. Iterating Based on Results

Metrics aren't static. AI projects evolve, and so should the ways you measure them:

- **Adjust Goals as Projects Scale**: Early pilots might focus on basic efficiency. Once stable, move to higher-level goals, like market expansion or brand enhancement.

- **Kill or Pivot Unsuccessful Projects**: If a project isn't meeting objectives, consider whether a pivot—or even a cancellation—is necessary. Resources might be better spent elsewhere.

- **Share Lessons Learned**: Document what succeeded, what failed, and what metrics were most revealing. This fosters organizational learning and shapes the criteria for future initiatives.

A Broader Definition of Success

After compiling a comprehensive report on AI's performance at 365 Strategies, Alex presented the findings to a small group of execs and department heads. Numbers were certainly there: proposals were drafted 30% faster, scheduling conflicts dropped by nearly half, and a pilot tool in Finance saved an estimated $50,000 in labor costs annually.

But what drew the most conversation was a section titled "Beyond the Numbers." Alex had included quotes from employees who felt more engaged now that busywork was automated. The report also cited an uptick in prospective client inquiries where AI solutions were specifically mentioned. "They've heard we're doing exciting things with AI," Alex explained. "They want to know what else we can help them with."

Jordan nodded, clearly impressed. "So, we're seeing both financial gains and a morale boost. That's a solid argument for continued investment."

One senior consultant chimed in: "It also positions us as a leader. We're not just a consulting firm—we're a firm that uses cutting-edge AI methods. Our reputation benefits."

In that moment, Alex realized the power of measuring AI success holistically. The "softer" benefits were at times just as persuasive as the hard data. By framing AI's value in a way that acknowledged both tangible ROI and intangible cultural shifts, Alex helped unify the group's perspective on the next wave of AI projects. Sure, numbers mattered—but the bigger story was how AI was reshaping 365 Strategies from the inside out.

OVERCOMING COMMON PITFALLS AND CHALLENGES

Facing Skepticism at 365 Strategies

Alex leaned back in their chair, noticing the uneasy expressions around the conference table. A new AI tool that promised to optimize client billing hours had been unveiled, and while it looked promising on paper, the finance team was nervous about data accuracy, and some consultants worried it might undermine their judgment when quoting projects. Jordan, seated at the head of the table, asked Alex directly, "How do we make sure this doesn't blow up in our faces? We can't afford a major mistake with client invoices."

Deep down, Alex understood their concerns. AI adoption at 365 Strategies had been transformative, but not everyone was fully on board. Some staff feared the technology might reduce their roles. Others had encountered glitches in earlier pilots—leading to skepticism about timeline promises or model reliability. Even Alex had wrestled with doubts when data hiccups threatened critical deadlines.

As the group voiced their worries, Alex recalled the many ups and downs of previous AI rollouts—some overcame challenges smoothly, others got stuck in friction. Reflecting on past experiences, Alex decided to approach this new project with a blend of honesty, open dialogue, and a deliberate rollout. "Let's address concerns head-on," Alex suggested, "and if we plan carefully, we can turn these potential pitfalls into learning opportunities."

Navigating AI's Most Common Roadblocks

AI projects can yield incredible benefits, but they come with a unique set of pitfalls. Below are typical challenges organizations face, along with practical strategies to overcome them.

1. Resistance to Change

What Happens: Some employees or managers fear AI will replace them or disrupt established routines. They might question why the company can't just continue "business as usual."

How to Overcome:

- **Transparent Communication**: Explain the "why" behind AI initiatives—how automating certain tasks frees people to tackle more strategic or creative work.

- **Involve Skeptics Early**: Invite those with concerns to pilot groups where they can see AI's benefits firsthand and shape the tool's development.

- **Celebrate Small Wins**: Highlight quick successes or employee testimonials showing how AI actually lightens workloads rather than making jobs obsolete.

2. Data Quality and Infrastructure Hiccups

What Happens: Incomplete or inconsistent data can derail AI models. Legacy systems may not integrate smoothly with new tools, leading to delays or inaccurate predictions.

How to Overcome:

- **Data Audits**: Regularly review and clean data to ensure it's accurate and up to date.

- **Pilot Projects**: Start small with limited datasets before scaling up, learning which data pipelines need the most attention.

- **Stakeholder Alignment**: Get buy-in from IT, finance, and other departments so they commit to maintaining data standards and infrastructure upgrades.

3. Unrealistic Timelines and Expectations

What Happens: Leaders might assume AI is a quick fix, only to discover the complexity of modeling, data engineering, and user feedback cycles. Projects stall or rush, yielding mediocre results.

How to Overcome:

- **Educate Stakeholders**: Emphasize that AI requires experimentation and iterative model tuning.

- **Build in Buffer Time**: Account for data processing, retraining models, and integrating user feedback in your project plan.

- **Frequent Check-Ins**: Use agile methods like sprints and regular demos to spot unrealistic goals early and adjust accordingly.

4. Fear of Job Displacement

What Happens: Employees might worry that automation tools will make their roles redundant, leading to morale problems or active resistance.

How to Overcome:

- **Upskilling Programs**: Offer training so staff can develop AI-related skills, repositioning them for more analytical or strategic roles.

- **Highlight Human Expertise**: Show that AI complements rather than replaces employees, giving them more time for high-value tasks.

- **Role Redefinition**: Work with HR to evolve job descriptions in a way that integrates AI rather than eliminates positions.

5. Model Bias and Ethical Concerns

What Happens: AI systems can inadvertently discriminate if they learn from biased data. Unintended ethical violations damage the organization's reputation.

How to Overcome:

- **Bias Audits**: Regularly test models to ensure they're not producing skewed outcomes.

- **Inclusive Data Samples**: Use diverse datasets that represent various demographics and scenarios.

- **Ethics Guidelines**: Create clear policies and review boards for AI projects to ensure responsible use of technology.

Turning Hiccups into Growth

At 365 Strategies, Alex took a step back and designed a "risk map" for the new billing AI project. Each potential stumbling block—from staff fears about losing control over quotes to data synchronization across multiple legacy systems—was noted, along with a plan to address it. Alex then scheduled open-door sessions for the finance and consulting teams, letting them see early prototypes of the billing AI tool and voice concerns in real time.

Some of the feedback was harsh—people pointed out clunky user interfaces and flagged scenarios the model didn't handle well. But Alex saw it as constructive. By surfacing these issues early, the team could refine the tool before it went live. Over a series of short sprints, they tweaked the user interface, cleaned up data pipelines, and even retrained parts of the model with more comprehensive records, improving accuracy.

A few weeks later, Jordan remarked on how smoothly the pilot was going, despite initial apprehensions. "We still had bumps, but it didn't derail us," he said, clearly pleased. The difference was that everyone felt their input had been heard. Those who once feared losing their roles now saw the AI tool as a partner—one that removed tedious billing checks, allowing them to focus on meaningful client interactions.

Alex couldn't help but smile at how something once seen as a "risk" had evolved into a showcase of cross-departmental collaboration. Reflecting on the broader journey, Alex understood that hurdles were normal—maybe even necessary for growth. By tackling obstacles head-on, offering transparency, and treating each glitch or fear as a learning moment, 365 Strategies continued to strengthen its AI capabilities and culture.

In the end, the process of overcoming challenges built more than just technical resilience; it built trust and confidence among staff. And that, Alex realized, was often the secret to sustaining an AI transformation: seeing problems not as dead ends, but as stepping stones toward a more adaptable, engaged, and innovation-ready organization.

PART V: LOOKING AHEAD AND SUSTAINING GROWTH

AI IN AN EVOLVING LANDSCAPE— TRENDS AND INNOVATIONS

A Revelatory Tech Expo

Alex stood in a bustling convention hall, weaving through a crowd of tech enthusiasts and industry professionals. Holographic displays advertised the latest in robotics, while a booth around the corner showcased advanced vision systems that could identify defects on an assembly line with near-perfect accuracy. At another stand, a startup demonstrated generative AI capable of designing rudimentary building layouts, drawing gasps from curious onlookers.

Attending this annual tech expo was an eye-opener for Alex. Though 365 Strategies had done a lot with AI already—automation, predictive scheduling, even generative content for proposals—this event highlighted just how rapidly the field was evolving. One presenter discussed new breakthroughs in machine learning that made it easier to fine-tune algorithms with far less data. Another teased next-gen robotics designed to collaborate seamlessly with human workers in everything from factories to hospitals.

While the excitement in the air was palpable, Alex remained pragmatic. "Which of these developments are actually relevant to 365 Strategies?" they wondered. Some tools looked too experimental, while others might complement existing consulting services. Jotting down notes, Alex felt an invigorating mix of awe and caution. The challenge now was to bring these insights back to the firm without chasing hype for hype's sake.

Staying Grounded in a Rapidly Evolving AI World

AI isn't a static discipline. It evolves daily, introducing fresh opportunities and challenges. For organizations hoping to leverage AI's latest and greatest, it's crucial to keep a pulse on emerging trends—while also using a discerning eye to avoid jumping into technology that isn't ready or relevant.

1. Key Emerging Trends

- **Generative Models**: Beyond text generation, AI can now create images, videos, even 3D designs. Such systems can spark new ideas in architecture, marketing, product design, and more. However, they also raise issues around authenticity and ethical use (e.g., deepfakes).

- **Advanced Computer Vision**: Camera-based AI isn't just for facial recognition anymore. From detecting microscopic flaws in products to analyzing complex medical imagery, vision-based models are becoming more accurate and affordable.

- **Robotics and Cobots**: Collaborative robots (cobots) work safely alongside human employees, performing tasks that require precision or repetitive motion. This technology is maturing, enabling broader use in warehouses, factories, and even restaurants.

- **Low-Code/No-Code AI Platforms**: Tools that let non-programmers build AI workflows with drag-and-drop interfaces. This democratizes AI but requires governance to ensure quality and security.

2. Evaluating Hype vs. Real Value

With so many headlines promising "the next big thing," it's easy to get carried away. Organizations must critically assess whether a new AI innovation:

- **Solves a Genuine Need**: Does it address an actual pain point or improve a core function?

- **Fits Current Capabilities**: Do you have the infrastructure and skill sets to deploy and maintain it?

- **Aligns with Strategic Goals**: Technology should serve the broader roadmap, not distract from it.

One approach is to adopt an innovation funnel—quickly prototype or research a technology in a limited setting, gather evidence, and decide if it warrants more investment.

3. Balancing Exploration and Caution

While skepticism helps avoid misguided projects, complete risk-aversion can stunt progress. Striking a balance means:

- **Designating an Innovation Team**: A small group can keep tabs on emerging tech, run feasibility studies, and recommend potential pilots without derailing core operations.

- **Setting a Budget for Experiments**: Allocate resources for pilot tests so promising ideas get a fair shot, but cap spending to manage risk.

- **Learning from Others**: Collaborate with universities, join industry consortia, or partner with startups to stay informed about cutting-edge developments.

4. Cultivating a Future-Ready Mindset

No one can predict exactly where AI will be in five years, but maintaining a future-oriented culture helps organizations adapt:

- **Continuous Learning**: Encourage ongoing skill development, from advanced analytics to product management for new AI services.

- **Open Communication**: Foster dialogues about emerging trends at all levels—from executives who shape long-term strategy to entry-level employees who see day-to-day opportunities.

- **Adaptable Structures**: Keep your organization flexible, with the ability to quickly pivot or scale AI initiatives as the tech improves.

Sharing Insights Back at 365 Strategies

Returning from the expo, Alex called an impromptu "tech briefing" in the cafeteria. Curious employees stopped by to hear about the futuristic demos Alex had witnessed. Over pastries and coffee, Alex explained the latest generative modeling breakthroughs and how advanced computer vision might soon detect even subtle irregularities in supply chains.

Some folks shrugged—feeling that 365 Strategies was a consulting firm, not a robotics manufacturer. But others' eyes lit up. A marketing lead imagined using generative design to craft hyper-personalized campaigns. An operations manager speculated about new AI tools that could refine resource allocation with data streaming in real time.

Yet Alex tempered the excitement with caution. "Not all of it is ready for prime time," they said. "We need to pick the gems that align with our goals and test them thoroughly." Jordan, who dropped by halfway through the conversation, agreed. "We've come a long way with AI, but let's stay strategic. No sense chasing every shiny object."

At the end of the briefing, Alex felt a renewed sense of optimism. Even though some cutting-edge technologies might not fit the firm immediately, staying curious kept them poised for the next evolution. By keeping an eye on what's emerging—and being willing to pilot new ideas in controlled ways—365 Strategies could maintain its forward-thinking edge. It was a lesson in balancing wonder and practicality: the AI landscape would keep evolving, but with the right mindset, the company could evolve right along with it.

SCALING BEYOND THE PILOT— ENTERPRISE-WIDE INTEGRATION

From Small Pilots to a Bigger Vision

Alex leaned back in a conference room chair at 365 Strategies, eyeing the collage of Post-it notes taped on the wall. Each sticky note represented an AI pilot—some already deemed successful, others mid-flight. From automated invoice checking to the proposal-generation tool, these projects had proven that AI could deliver value in scattered pockets of the company. Now, Jordan and other leaders were asking a new question: "How do we weave AI into the fabric of 365 Strategies, rather than treating it as a one-off experiment?"

A lively discussion ensued among department heads. The marketing team wanted to expand its predictive tools to every client campaign. Operations proposed deeper data integrations to unify scheduling with resource allocation firm-wide. Finance hoped to incorporate AI-driven forecasts for long-term budgeting. Alex sensed the collective ambition, but also the risk: if each team pursued AI solutions independently, they might reinvent the wheel or create conflicting systems.

Looking at the enthusiastic but somewhat scattered ideas, Alex realized it was time for a more systematic approach. "What if we created a centralized 'AI Hub'?" they proposed. "A resource to share best practices, maintain standards, and help each department implement AI responsibly." The response was immediate, with nods of agreement. Excitement filled the room as they recognized that scaling AI beyond pilots could unlock massive collaborative potential—if done correctly.

Keys to Successful Enterprise AI Integration

Taking AI from a few pilot projects to organization-wide adoption involves more than replicating small successes. It requires a governance framework, shared infrastructure, and a supportive culture that aligns teams around common goals. Below are the critical steps to ensure a seamless and scalable AI rollout.

1. Establish Clear Governance and Oversight

As AI spreads, oversight becomes essential to prevent duplication and maintain quality:

- **Dedicated AI Committee**: Form a cross-functional body (HR, IT, Finance, Operations, etc.) to review new AI proposals, set priorities, and approve resources.

- **Standards and Guidelines**: Document coding standards, model evaluation criteria, and ethical considerations. This ensures consistent quality across different teams.

- **Transparent Approval Process**: Define how teams can propose new AI initiatives and how resources will be allocated. This promotes fairness and discourages siloed projects.

A strong governance structure provides guardrails so AI initiatives align with overarching company objectives rather than scattering in every direction.

2. Centralize Data and Infrastructure

When multiple departments leverage AI, fragmented data can become a major bottleneck. A unified approach helps:

- **Shared Data Lake or Warehouse**: Store key datasets in one secure, accessible location. This prevents duplication of data efforts and allows cross-departmental insights.

- **Common Tools and Platforms**: Standardize on a few AI frameworks or cloud platforms to simplify collaboration and reduce maintenance overhead.

- **Scalable Architecture**: Plan for increased data volume and model complexity. Evaluate whether cloud solutions or on-premises expansions best fit your anticipated growth.

By providing consistent technical resources, the organization can accelerate AI deployments without reinventing the wheel each time.

3. Create an "AI Hub" or Center of Excellence

To facilitate knowledge-sharing, establish a centralized AI resource center:

- **Best Practices Repository**: Document successful models, lessons learned, and success stories.
- **Internal Training and Workshops**: Offer regular sessions to upskill employees across departments, ensuring a baseline understanding of AI's capabilities.
- **Expert Consultants**: Assign data scientists or AI leads who can rotate through various projects, ensuring consistent quality and mentoring teams with less experience.

This hub acts as both a support system and an innovation engine, preventing AI from becoming scattered or siloed.

4. Manage the Cultural Transition

Scaling AI isn't just about technology; it's a cultural shift:

- **Leadership Support**: Executives should champion AI, making it clear it's a strategic priority, not a passing trend.
- **Open Communication**: Encourage teams to share progress, roadblocks, and feedback openly. A Slack channel, weekly newsletter, or town hall Q&A can keep everyone informed and engaged.

- **Recognition of Success**: Celebrate milestones publicly—like the first department to fully integrate AI or the biggest measured efficiency boost—so employees feel motivated and appreciated.

The goal is to ensure that employees see AI not as an isolated set of tools, but as an integral part of the company's evolution.

5. Expect Complexity—and Growth

When multiple teams deploy AI, complexities inevitably arise:

- **Overlapping Projects**: Two departments might aim for similar solutions, leading to confusion or wasted effort. The AI Hub can mediate and unify these efforts.

- **Scaling Challenges**: A model that worked with one department's data may strain under a broader dataset, requiring retraining or architectural changes.

- **Continuous Improvement**: Enterprise AI is never "done." Ongoing updates, performance monitoring, and dataset expansions mean the work evolves over time.

Still, these complexities bring opportunities for synergy. Departments can share data insights, cross-fertilize ideas, and push each other toward higher levels of AI maturity.

Building the AI Hub at 365 Strategies

After the initial brainstorming on scaling AI, Alex formed a small committee—dubbed the "AI Task Force"—consisting of representatives from different departments. Their first major initiative was to create a blueprint for a centralized AI Hub. This hub would store model templates, data pipelines, and best practices. It also included a roadmap for how new AI proposals would be vetted and integrated.

In parallel, IT set up a shared cloud environment, consolidating key datasets in a well-organized data warehouse. Marketing started eyeing the repository for consumer insights, while Operations eagerly anticipated connecting their scheduling tool to real-time data feeds from other departments.

Some hurdles cropped up. For instance, data scientists had to carefully manage version control for models as multiple teams sought to tailor them. A few employees, already swamped with daily tasks, worried about learning yet another system. But Alex and the committee tackled these concerns with patient communication and hands-on training sessions. They explained that the AI Hub would actually reduce duplication, freeing employees to focus on what they did best.

Within months, the benefits were tangible. Departments collaborated on AI ideas instead of working in isolation. A quick meeting with the AI Hub could confirm whether a model existed or if additional data was available to enhance a new solution. Pilot success rates improved, and the leadership team enjoyed a clear view of how AI projects laddered up to broader strategic goals.

One afternoon, Jordan commended Alex on the new structure. "We're beyond the pilot stage," he said, tapping the AI Hub's dashboard on a large screen. "Now we have a real system—one that helps us harness AI's potential across every corner of the firm."

Alex left that meeting feeling both relieved and proud. Scaling had brought new layers of complexity, but it had also enabled a cultural shift: AI was no longer a series of experiments but a unifying force. Watching different teams collaborate under a common framework hinted at the massive potential 365 Strategies could unlock in the coming months. It felt as though they'd just taken another crucial step in turning AI from a novelty into a core strength that would keep the firm competitive and innovative for years to come.

BUILDING A SUSTAINABLE AI FUTURE— ETHICAL LEADERSHIP AND RESPONSIBILITY

A Crossroads of Morals and Technology

Alex glanced over a draft policy document labeled "Ethical AI Guidelines—365 Strategies." After months of implementing AI solutions—from automated proposals to predictive analytics—leadership had tasked Alex with ensuring that these tools remained a force for good. The document contained sections on data privacy, transparency, fairness, and user accountability. Yet, as Alex read through it, they realized just how deep this topic went.

At a recent internal meeting, a heated debate had erupted when someone raised a scenario: what if the AI's recommendations unintentionally discriminated against certain clients or job applicants? Another colleague pointed out the potential fallout if a flawed AI model made significant billing errors. "These aren't just technical snafus," Alex had said. "They're ethical dilemmas that could damage our reputation and hurt real people."

Jordan, who had been championing AI adoption, nodded grimly. "We want to be leaders in AI, but not at the cost of integrity. We need clear guidelines now, before something goes wrong and we're forced to react." Alex took the hint and began crafting a policy that went beyond mere compliance. This wasn't just about following laws; it was about upholding values that would sustain AI's long-term role in the company.

Foundations of Ethical AI and Responsible Leadership

As AI grows more powerful, organizations must ensure that their innovations serve the greater good, not just the bottom line. This requires deliberate leadership and robust frameworks that prioritize ethics, transparency, and continual oversight.

1. Why Ethical AI Matters

- **Public Trust**: Misuse of data or biased AI systems can erode customer confidence. Trust, once broken, is hard to rebuild.

- **Avoiding Harm**: Even unintentional errors—like a loan approval algorithm that excludes certain groups—can cause real harm to individuals or communities.

- **Long-Term Innovation**: Ethical considerations foster innovation that's sustainable. When employees and clients trust AI, they're more open to experimenting and scaling solutions.

An ethical AI approach goes beyond checking a compliance box. It underpins the organization's reputation, customer relationships, and capacity for future growth.

2. Core Principles of an Ethical AI Framework

1. **Fairness and Inclusivity**

   - **Avoid Bias**: Regularly test models for discriminatory outcomes, retrain if biases emerge.

   - **Diverse Data**: Use broad, inclusive datasets that represent multiple demographics and use cases.

2. **Transparency and Explainability**

   - **Explainable Outcomes**: Where feasible, choose AI methods that allow stakeholders to understand why a model reached a certain decision.

   - **Honest Communication**: If using AI for customer-facing decisions (like credit approvals), clarify how the process works and what data is used.

3. **Privacy and Security**

- Data Minimization: Collect only the data needed, store it securely, and respect user opt-outs.

- Robust Safeguards: Encrypt sensitive info and monitor systems to catch breaches or suspicious activities swiftly.

4. **Accountability and Governance**

- Clear Responsibility: Identify who's accountable when AI systems err—be it a model owner, project lead, or governance committee.

- Ongoing Audits: Conduct periodic reviews to ensure the AI continues meeting ethical standards as data and use cases evolve.

5. **User-Centric Design**

- Human Oversight: High-stakes decisions (like hiring or medical diagnoses) should still involve human review.

- Accessible Feedback Loops: Let users report anomalies or concerns so that AI can improve over time.

These principles create a foundation that goes well beyond simple compliance, embedding ethical thinking into day-to-day operations.

3. Operationalizing Ethical AI

Ethical guidelines only work if people actually follow them:

- **Ethics Committees or Boards**: Form a cross-functional team to evaluate new AI proposals, ensuring they align with the company's standards.

- **Documented Processes**: Maintain clear records of model objectives, training data, and update histories. This transparency helps if questions or conflicts arise later.

- **Employee Training**: Host sessions so everyone understands ethical considerations. This is especially critical for developers, data scientists, and anyone who labels or curates data.

By ingraining ethics into each step—from ideation to deployment—the organization builds a culture where responsible AI is second nature.

4. Continuous Monitoring and Improvement

AI systems aren't static; they learn and adapt. That's why ethical leadership doesn't end at launch:

- **Ongoing Model Reviews**: Schedule monthly or quarterly check-ins to test for new biases or performance drifts.

- **Incident Response Plans**: Define how to handle ethics or security breaches, including how to communicate with affected customers and regulators.

- **Stakeholder Engagement**: Seek periodic feedback from employees, clients, and external experts. Fresh perspectives can highlight blind spots and drive refinements.

This continuous loop—monitor, evaluate, refine—keeps AI usage aligned with evolving societal norms and organizational values.

A Policy that Shapes the Future

After several weeks of collecting feedback from departments and legal advisors, Alex presented the final "Ethical AI Guidelines" to the leadership council at 365 Strategies. The policy contained practical requirements—like bias checks and data handling procedures—but also a statement of core values emphasizing fairness, transparency, and respect for individual privacy.

To implement the policy, Alex proposed creating a small "Ethics and Oversight" subcommittee. Its members would be drawn from IT, legal, marketing, and even an external advisor with experience in digital ethics.

This group would periodically review existing AI tools, greenlight new initiatives, and maintain a direct line of communication for staff who spotted potential issues.

During the discussion, one department head worried about adding bureaucracy. "Won't this slow us down?" they asked. "We need to remain competitive."

Alex acknowledged the concern but countered, "If our AI accidentally steps on ethical landmines, the fallout could slow us down much more. A well-defined policy helps us innovate responsibly, not fearfully." Jordan nodded in agreement, recognizing that a small overhead in oversight was worth the assurance that 365 Strategies wouldn't undermine its reputation or harm customers.

In the weeks after the policy rollout, Alex noticed a tangible shift in attitudes. Employees felt more comfortable speaking up if they spotted data anomalies or unclear model results. Clients appreciated the firm's proactive stance, and some even started asking if 365 Strategies could help them develop their own ethical AI strategies.

Reflecting on the journey, Alex realized that responsibility was more than a corporate buzzword; it was the bedrock of sustainable AI adoption. By leading with integrity and transparency, 365 Strategies was setting itself up not just for short-term gains, but for a future where technology and humanity coexisted in a way that honored both progress and principles.

REFLECTION, NEXT STEPS, AND FINAL THOUGHTS

AI's Journey from Simple Tasks to Strategic Transformation

Sitting in a quiet corner of the 365 Strategies office, Alex flipped through a dog-eared notebook containing scribbles from when the AI journey first began. Once upon a time, "AI" felt like a buzzword, or at best, a distant possibility. The firm's earliest projects were small but significant—simple automations that saved a handful of hours each week. It was the Ground Floor stage of the GAIN model, where the biggest leaps involved learning to trust that AI could handle routine tasks.

From there, the company advanced to using AI in more robust ways, optimizing workflows and cutting errors. The Advance stage brought efficiency improvements that made day-to-day operations faster and more precise. Employees started seeing AI not as a novelty, but as a genuine partner in their work.

When 365 Strategies reached Innovate, everything shifted. AI was no longer about incremental gains; it became a spark for reimagining how proposals were created, how projects were scheduled, and how data was gathered. Processes themselves were transformed, proving that AI could be a catalyst for genuinely new solutions.

Finally, the firm ventured into New Horizons, launching platform-based offerings that transcended traditional consulting. AI no longer just supported the business—it helped redefine it, creating new revenue streams and cementing 365 Strategies' reputation as an industry leader.

Through each step—Ground Floor, Advance, Innovate, and New Horizons—the company met obstacles: skeptical colleagues, messy data, tight deadlines, and ethical dilemmas. Yet each challenge encouraged them to refine their vision, rally collaborative teams, and reinforce the importance of responsible AI leadership.

Vision, Teamwork, and Continuous Learning

The story of AI at 365 Strategies holds several universal lessons, beneficial for any organization stepping onto this path:

1. **Start Small, But Start**
   Even the biggest AI transformations begin with modest pilot projects. These early "quick wins" help teams build confidence and learn the fundamentals without sinking too many resources at once.

2. **Align AI with Real Goals**
   Technology for technology's sake rarely works. By connecting AI to tangible objectives—be it reducing errors, boosting sales, or discovering new markets—leaders can gather support, secure budgets, and measure true impact.

3. **Embrace Collaboration and a Learning Culture**
   AI crosses departmental lines, requiring data scientists, domain experts, and project managers to work in unison. Investing in upskilling and open communication prevents AI from becoming a "black box" understood by only a handful of tech-savvy individuals.

4. **Prioritize Ethics and Responsibility**
   With great power comes the need for oversight and integrity. Setting standards, regularly auditing algorithms, and maintaining transparency protect both the organization and its stakeholders from unintended harm.

5. **Celebrate Milestones and Look Ahead**
   Each stage of AI maturity—Ground Floor to New Horizons— brings its own triumphs. Recognizing these achievements fuels morale and keeps teams enthusiastic about the road still ahead.

By weaving these principles into organizational fabric, AI ceases to be a daunting frontier. Instead, it becomes a sustainable, evolving strength.

Looking to the Future

In a final leadership meeting, Alex pulled together the heads of every department, from Finance to Operations to Marketing. They walked through a concise presentation that recapped the four stages of the GAIN model, highlighting how each department's AI projects contributed to 365 Strategies' overall growth. Colorful charts showed time saved, improvements in client satisfaction, and new revenue sources from AI-driven offerings.

Jordan rose from his seat once the presentation concluded. "It's astonishing how far we've come," he said, scanning the room. "Not that long ago, we were talking about simple data-entry automation. Now we're launching AI products, winning new clients, and exploring partnerships we never dreamed of."

Nods and smiles rippled around the table. Some recalled the early skepticism—would AI actually help, or was it just hype? Others reflected on all the hurdles: data hiccups, ethical quandaries, clashing priorities. But together, they'd navigated each challenge, maturing from AI novices to responsible innovators.

As the team wrapped up, Alex felt an odd mix of pride and anticipation. The GAIN model might have guided them here, but the journey was far from over. AI technologies continued to evolve, and so would 365 Strategies. Already, employees were floating ideas about next-generation analytics, personalized client dashboards, and advanced real-time market analysis.

Stepping out of the boardroom, Alex paused to reflect. Success with AI wasn't about a singular breakthrough—it was about persistence, teamwork, and continuous adaptation. The firm would keep exploring fresh avenues for AI, yet their commitment to careful strategy and ethical principles would remain non-negotiable.

And that's the final message to anyone venturing into AI: this journey has no true endpoint. Rather than waiting for a magical spark, organizations that thrive with AI blend vision, learning, and responsibility. By staying open to possibilities and refining what's already in place, you can harness AI's power to continually reshape your operations—and maybe even your entire industry.

From automating a few tasks to reinventing business models, AI can be a force of transformation, provided it's approached with clarity, heart, and an unwavering sense of purpose. Alex and the team at 365 Strategies had proven that much. Now, as they looked ahead, they carried both the lessons of the past and the excitement for what was yet to come, ready to embark on the next evolution of AI's endless potential.